To [illegible]

We were [illegible] this was your great interest!

Happy hunting!

Xmas 1987 in Johannesburg, South Africa

Steph & Chris Marsh

MEETING WITH BIRDS

One hundred birds to know

Tom Spence

with field sketches by Clive Hopcroft

DELTA BOOKS

DELTA BOOKS (PTY) LTD
A subsidiary of Donker Holdings (Pty) Ltd
P O Box 41021
Craighall
2024

© Tom Spence, 1986

All rights reserved. No part of this publication
may be reproduced, stored in a retrieval system,
or transmitted in any form or by any means, electronic,
mechanical, photocopying, or otherwise, without
the prior permission of the publisher.

First published 1986

ISBN 0 908387 60 1

Set in 11/12 Times Roman by Fotoplate
Printed and bound by Creda Press (Pty) Ltd, Cape Town

Contents

Acknowledgements	6
Introduction	7
How to use this book well	8
Descriptive groupings	9
One hundred birds	19
Index	119

Acknowledgements

A book comes into being as the result of an idea; *Meeting with Birds* was the idea of Adriaan Donker, who perceived the need for a less formal approach to birdwatching. Recognition rather than identification would be the criterion.

Could I ever hope to secure a place in a field so thoroughly covered by a multitude of books about birds, was my first reaction. Yet as this book came together I realised that Adriaan was right. His encouragement and enthusiasm have been echoed by many other people. To all these people go my thanks for motivating me to complete this book when time was against me.

My wife, Anne, endured the birthpains of the book with newfound patience, especially when keys clacked far into the night. Each *bird* that emerged from the wordprocessor was scrutinised and analysed for its suitability to the informal watcher (which Anne, of course, is).

Clive Hopcroft made the field sketches in record time, generously including an extra twenty to cope with my indecision on the final one hundred. Clive's ideas and suggestions have proved invaluable.

Norman Elwell is the major contributor of photographs; more than forty come from his own collection. I sincerely appreciate the support I have had from Norman over many years.

Geoff McIlleron contributed substantially to the photographs and provided the leads for those he did not have.

Bird photographers Geoff Lockwood, Peter Barachievy, Peter Ginn, Nico Myburgh and the late Will Nichol are all represented within the pages of this book.

Each one of these people has added something and I am grateful to them all.

Introduction

You don't have to be a botanist to appreciate flowers, nor a musician to savour the beauty of sound. You don't have to be an ornithologist to enjoy birds – perhaps the most appealing of all wild creatures. Yet without an introduction, formal or informal, many rewarding moments would be lost. We simply wouldn't realise what gifts of nature existed.

How many lovers of the outdoors miss the gems that lie in their path through lack of guidance? How many subtle bird-sounds are lost to the untrained ear in the varied orchestral overture to each day?

This book aims to capture in picture and print those vital first impressions which strike the senses when meeting with a particular bird, and which make the meeting interesting and rewarding. You the reader are given the opportunity to lock some of these details in your memory; ready for the day when you meet up with one or more of the birds described in this book.

You may find yourself noticing the Blackshouldered Kite hovering above the freeway as you drive to work. You could easily start scanning dams for dabchicks and categorise the resident birds in your garden into a dozen species or more. Every one of the 100 species of birds presented can be seen in most parts of the country.

The meetings may be intimate, where a wild creature has set aside its fear to make your garden its home. The encounter may be more formal, where you eye each other at a discreet distance – you are the invader; your behaviour could so easily destroy that reserved tolerance accorded to you. Or the meeting may be one-sided, your presence at the interface of two environments going unnoticed. You are a mere speck to the members of the vast V-formation of ibises disappearing into the evening sky. Yet even these meetings may bring much pleasure and may sometimes be quite moving.

This bird-guide differs from most other guides in that it is neither a comprehensive work of reference nor just a book of pretty bird pictures. It is an aid to condition yourself to see birds and to identify them by the impression they make on you. Use this book lightly and enjoy the results. Serious bird-watching can come later if you would like it to.

How to use this book well

This book is designed to lead you into bird identification gently, by the subjective grouping of selected birds. Locality has not been the sole criterion for grouping birds. Instead characteristics which they have in common have been considered. These could be the sharing of habitat, familial relationships – or classification based on the author's empirical logic. Birds you are likely to see on a seaside holiday for example, are collectively described as 'White Birds of the Sea and Shore'. There follows a short comment on these birds to add more colour to the picture, then a list of the birds in that grouping, which are more fully written up and illustrated in the body of the book. It is recommended that you familiarise yourself with a grouping before exploring the section of the book where individual birds falling into that group are described.

When you get to the description page do a quick check against the colour code to see where the bird is found. (Red indicates Transvaal; Blue, the Cape; Yellow, Orange Free State; and Green, Natal.) This will immediately tell you whether the bird occurs regularly in the place where you happen to be. Look at the colour picture and absorb the image of the bird, then glance at the sketch which presents a typical pose.

Now read the text to bring life to the visual impressions by sharing the author's view of the bird, which is based on many meetings.

If you wish to explore further, check the 'Roberts number' (e.g. R104) and then go to *Roberts' Birds of Southern Africa*, 5th edition, 1984. The numbers do not coincide with earlier editions of *Roberts* and some names have changed.

If you are having difficulty in identifying a bird which doesn't quite fit a description in this book, look at the list of birds which look similar and again refer to *Roberts*. This will also help you expand your knowledge of birds.

However, you need go no further than the pages of this small book to savour the delights of our birds.

Descriptive Groupings

1 White Birds of the Sea and Shore
Gannets, gulls and terns.
These are the birds one associates with curling, green waves breaking on rocks, leaving pools behind. Gulls and terns are related, gannets are the odd birds out; but they all share the sea as a source of food.

Birds described:
1 Kelp Gull
2 Greyheaded Gull
3 Cape Gannet

2 Divers of Inland Waters
Coots, cormorants and dabchicks.
Almost every dam or pan is fitted out with these three very different diving birds. Each species is efficiently designed to use the resources of their habitat in their own specific way.

Birds described:
4 Dabchick
5 Reed Cormorant
6 Redknobbed Coot

3 Long-necked Stalkers of Veld and Vlei
Herons and egrets.
They all belong to one big family, but each has its own idea about making a living. Although designed to stand in water and spear frogs, some herons and egrets have settled for dry-land feeding on mice, lizards and insects.

Birds described:
7 Grey Heron
8 Blackheaded Heron
9 Cattle Egret

4 The Brown Enigma
Hamerkop.
A lone species of Africa with no near relatives, the Hamerkop is as drab as the mud in which it feeds. This bird's unusual nest and subversive appearance have linked it with superstitious beliefs.

Bird described:
10 Hamerkop

5 Big-billed Striders
Storks, cranes and ibises.

These are big birds, very different yet often confused. Cranes are elegant up-market creatures; a complement to an ornamental garden. Storks are modest birds with long, often coloured, straight bills. Not all present the fairy-tale image. Ibises are working-class birds with long, curved bills and few pretensions.

Birds described:
11 White Stork
12 Abdim's Stork
13 Blue Crane
14 Sacred Ibis
15 Hadeda Ibis

6 Filter-feeders on Stilts
Flamingoes.

Flamingoes are one of the extremes in bird design; who would have thought of raising a bird on long, long legs and then making it feed by filtering water with its head upside down. Gathered in their hundreds and even thousands they are a spectacular display.

Bird described:
16 Greater Flamingo

7 Water-loving Game Birds
Ducks and geese.

Ducks and water are universally associated and our ducks are no exception. Geese are part of the family. Our males do not generally adopt the gaudy breeding fashions of Northern Hemisphere counterparts.

Birds described:
17 Egyptian Goose
18 Yellowbilled Duck

8 An Eagle on Foot
Secretary Bird.

A unique all-African species designed for striding across the veld instead of soaring as many other birds of prey do.

Bird described:
19 Secretary Bird

9 Hunters from the Sky
Vultures, hawks and eagles.
These are the birds of prey that hunt by day. Spread over several families, this group takes in all from the big, hunched vultures, the noble eagles and the languid buzzards; to the smaller, high-speed falcons, hawks and kestrels.

Birds described:
20 Cape Vulture
21 Blackshouldered Kite
22 Black Eagle
23 African Fish Eagle

10 Ground-loving Wildfowl
Francolins, guineafowl and korhaans.
These birds share the open-veld niche. First introductions may be the sudden release of a feathered missile beneath your feet. The korhaan is the most flamboyant of these ground birds. Francolins and guineafowl share a chicken-like approach to finding food.

Birds described:
24 Coqui Francolin
25 Swainson's Francolin
26 Helmeted Guineafowl
27 Black Korhaan

11 Runners on Dry Land and Wet
Plovers and dikkops.
Plovers patrol veld and vlei during the day; dikkops take over at night. Long legs lift these medium-sized birds enough to see over short grass and help them skulk away quickly when danger approaches. Both nest on the ground and are very aggressive.

Birds described:
28 Threebanded Plover
29 Crowned Plover
30 Spotted Dikkop

12 Ubiquitous Birds that Coo
Doves and pigeons.
Symbol of peace, carriers of messages and messers of statues, the family needs no introduction. The division into doves and pigeons is dependent on size and colour. Aggression is a characteristic of the doves.

Birds described:
31 Rock Pigeon
32 Cape Turtle Dove
33 Laughing Dove

13 Tree-bound Curiosities
Louries.
These birds of contrast are either brilliantly coloured in red, green, purple and blue; or are an unassuming grey. All of them run about branches with a clockwork agility as they seek their daily fare of fruits and seeds.

Bird described:
34 Grey Lourie

14 Traditional Parasites and Relatives
Cuckoos and coucals.
Cuckoos, both the sombre and glossy species, lay their eggs in other birds' nests and have no further interest in their young. Coucals uphold parental duties on their side of the family and even feed their young on the offspring of other birds.

Birds described:
35 Red-chested Cuckoo
36 Diederik Cuckoo
37 Burchell's Coucal

15 Night-time Hunters and Associates
Owls and nightjars.
Owls are raptors in beak and claw; nightjars are mild, wide-mouthed moth traps with almost no beak at all and legs that are barely more than a soft-landing device. Their only claim to association is a shareholding in the night and some overlap of habitat.

Birds described:
38 Barn Owl
39 Pearlspotted Owl
40 Spotted Eagle Owl
41 Fierynecked Nightjar

16 Crescent-winged Fliers and Similar
Swifts and swallows.
Swifts are modestly coloured masters of the air with little claim to land; swallows are gentler birds in flight and manner, often with glossy blue plumage to contrast russet and white. Both take their food on the move in the air.

Birds described:
42 Whiterumped Swift
43 European Swallow
44 Lesser Striped Swallow

17 Mouse-like Lovers of Fruit
Mousebirds.
Any similarity with any mouse alive or dead is purely coincidental. Operating in gangs, mousebirds ravage cultivated fruit which has no doubt led to their widespread distribution.

Bird described:
45 Speckled Mousebird

18 Fishers Genuine and Modified
Kingfishers.
They are well-equipped with a generous and sharp bill, to take fish from the water by diving. Yet some have forsaken this way of life, perhaps disillusioned by drought, to live off insects. Not all conform to the traditional, colourful, biscuit-tin image.

Birds described:
46 Pied Kingfisher
47 Malachite Kingfisher
48 Brownhooded Kingfisher

19 Elegant Hawkers of Bees and Kin
Bee-eaters.
In graceful flight or perched on some prominent point, bee-eaters rank among our most beautiful birds. Green, yellow, blue and even carmine have been generously splashed in this elegant family. As if to multiply their magnificence some bee-eaters flock together in their hundreds.

Bird described:
49 Little Bee-eater

20 Brilliant Blue Sentinels of the Bush
Rollers.
Rollers cannot easily be missed, for they are not shy in their choice of perch. Some show brilliant blue in flight which contrasts sharply with the drab bush habitat. Rollers take their name from their aerobatic courtship displays.

Bird described:
50 Lilacbreasted Roller

21 The Long Beak and Head-dress Theme
Hoopoes and woodhoopoes.
The hoopoes and woodhoopoes share a name but not a family; they differ greatly. The hoopoe must probe the soil for its food and wear a chieftain's head-dress; the woodhoopoe probes spiders from bark and sports glossy black plumage with white trim.

Birds described:
51 Hoopoe
52 Redbilled Woodhoopoe

22 Bills, Bills and more Bills
Hornbills.
Bills, with or without casque, coloured or plain, are a feature of this family, which with one exception live in trees. The female, in most species, is sealed in a tree-hole nest and relies on her mate to feed her through a narrow slit until the nestlings hatch.

Birds described:
53 Yellowbilled Hornbill
54 Ground Hornbill

23 Peckers of Wood and Beneficiaries
Barbets, woodpeckers and wrynecks.
All have a share in the tree-boring business, but only the barbets and woodpeckers are active partners. Wrynecks take over holes when the others move out. Barbets, woodpeckers and wrynecks belong to separate families, and differ markedly in design and habits.

Birds described:
55 Blackcollared Barbet
56 Crested Barbet
57 Cardinal Woodpecker
58 Redthroated Wryneck

24 Buffy Brown Songsters
Larks.
Locally manufactured versions of the sweet songster immortalised in numerous poems, our larks, twenty and more species of them, sing to the brown veld from some prominent perch or while flying up into the blue dome of the sky.

Bird described:
59 Rufousnaped Lark

25 Aggressive Mimics of Farm and Garden
Drongoes.
A conspicuous addition to your garden-bird repertoire, its presence will be felt by every cat, crow and other predator real or imagined. Nevertheless, a charming rogue to have around.

Bird described:
60 Forktailed Drongo

26 Golden Whistlers of Big-treed Gardens
Orioles.
The first introduction may be a sweet, liquid call coming from the canopy of a large tree. Later you may see the characteristic golden yellow of the caller as it shyly comes into view before flying swiftly away.

Bird described:
61 Blackheaded Oriole

27 Raucous Associates of Man
Crows and ravens.
They are swaggering black birds that loiter about the highways and rubbish dumps in small groups. More often seen flying to the accompaniment of harsh calls.

Bird described:
62 Pied Crow

28 Gregarious Noise-makers of the Thickets
Babblers.
They creep about almost unnoticed until one sets the rowdy chorus going, perhaps in response to the presence of an owl. Having hurled abuse they creep and fly away, momentarily silent and unobtrusive.

Bird described:
63 Arrowmarked Babbler

29 Cheerful Commoners in Residence
Bulbuls.
Every garden has one, although their appearance may vary slightly from one part of the country to another. In a friendly way they will advise you that they are there, and while they are at it, report on the presence of cats, snakes, owls and other predators.

Bird described:
64 Blackeyed Bulbul

30 Modest Residents of Bush and Garden
Thrushes, chats and robins.
They walk, perch or hop in a variety of habitats, and behave as though they did not all belong to one family. Appearance, too, varies between the members, but they all do agree that insects are food.

Birds described:
65 Kurrichane Thrush
66 Familiar Chat
67 Cape Robin

31 Small Dwellers of Scrub and Woodland
Titbabblers, prinias and warblers.
Some of the little birds in this group travel incognito in dull plumage and defy the most adept of bird-watchers to recognise them in the field. The distinction between titbabblers, prinias and warblers is however clear; and an appreciation of each is rewarding without having to delve too deep.

Birds described:
68 Titbabbler
69 Neddicky
70 Blackchested Prinia

32 Feathered Flycatching Friends of the Gardener
Flycatchers.
Appropriately these birds catch insects in flight, operating from a convenient perch. They range from the drab to startlingly beautiful in manner and appearance. Some adopt a 'doorstep' familiarity in their selection of a nesting site near the house.

Birds described:
71 Fiscal Flycatcher
72 Paradise Flycatcher

33 Garden Tail-waggers and Rural Kin
Wagtails, pipits and longclaws.
Wagtails are distinctive in manner and plumage. Longclaws too stand out in the monochrome of the veld. But pipits in dull-coloured plumage confuse. All three share a preference for walking rather than hopping.

Birds described:
73 Cape Wagtail
74 Richard's Pipit
75 Orangethroated Longclaw

34 Urban Hangmen and Bush Relatives
Shrikes.
They vary from the fiercely domineering garden bird to a beautiful bush recluse. Some are highly vocal and specialise in duets. All take insects as a major part of their diet.

Birds described:
76 Fiscal Shrike
77 Crimsonbreasted Shrike
78 Bokmakierie

35 City-dwelling Imports
Mynahs and starlings.
Aided by modified man-made habitats, these foreign squatters have displaced some more refined local residents and not much can be done about it.

Birds described:
79 European Starling
80 Indian Mynah

36 Shiny Birds of Bush and Garden
Starlings.
They all share shimmering plumage and a taste for fruit. In some, the adornment is confined to the male, in others there is little difference. Most are able to adapt to man-modified environments.

Birds described:
81 Plumcoloured Starling
82 Glossy Starling
83 Redwinged Starling

37 Gamecreepers of the Wild
Oxpeckers.
Exclusively designed to creep upon the backs and bellies of the big game, they have nevertheless adapted to cattle in some rural areas. They are the real tick-eating birds of Africa.

Bird described:
84 Redbilled Oxpecker

38 Nectar-loving Flower Birds
Sunbirds, sugarbirds and white-eyes.
A taste for sweetness brings representatives from three different families together. One of the three is bound to proteas as a source of food. The others are highly adaptable to various habitats.

Birds described:
85 Cape Sugarbird
86 Whitebellied Sunbird
87 Black Sunbird
88 Cape White-eye

39 Seed-eaters in the Garden
Sparrows and weavers.
Similar in manner but often different in appearance and nest-building, they both belong to a very big family. Plumage varies from dull city greys and browns to brilliant yellow in summer.

Birds described:
89 Cape Sparrow
90 Cape Weaver
91 Masked Weaver

40 Summertime Bishops and Widows of the Vlei
Bishops and widow birds.
Gorgeous males – some in black with tails to sport, some in fiery red or yellow with funereal trim, some with gold, white or red epaulettes – these are the showmen of the marsh. Here they woo drab mates until the calendar strikes April and finery fades to match the dry winter brown of the veld.

Birds described:
92 Red Bishop
93 Golden Bishop
94 Redcollared Widow
95 Longtailed Widow

41 Little Birds of the Grass
Waxbills.
As widespread as the grass seeds upon which they feed, these tiny off-cuts of Creation move in colourful flocks. Still much prized as cage-birds, they are now protected by a system of permits. Males and females adopt more or less unisex attire.

Birds described:
96 Blue Waxbill
97 Common Waxbill

42 Polygamous Parasites at your Feeding Tray
Whydahs.
Aggressively territorial, polygamous in the extreme, a brood parasite – these are some of the charges laid at the whydah's door. Long tails and a special plumage for the males in summer are what nature has specified.

Bird described:
98 Pintailed Whydah

43 Mellow Songsters of Garden and the Wild
Canaries and buntings.
Relatives of domesticated songsters, this family is one of the few that are sweetly vocal. Colours vary from traditional yellows and greeny shades to reddish browns, blacks and whites.

Birds described:
99 Yelloweyed Canary
100 Rock Bunting

1 Kelp Gull

Larus dominicanus
R312

Similar birds
Blackbrowed Albatross R12
Greyheaded Gull R315

During your first meeting you will share a habitat briefly. You may even be regarded as a source of food, especially if you are fishing. Heavy yellow bill with red tip and bold white and black plumage of the Kelp Gull impart an air of authority which you cannot ignore. In flight this gull is leisurely, as if on holiday, like you may be. At rest it is almost a fixture in the traditional seaside scene.

The Kelp Gull is an aggressive scavenger on land and over the water, and readily stoops to raiding rubbish dumps. It will also follow boats far out to sea, ready to pick up any scraps thrown overboard.

The Kelp Gull nests at ground level on rocky islands and on ledges of cliffs. Pebbles, seaweed, feathers and other odds and ends are scraped together to accommodate two or three blotchy eggs which will change to little gulls in about a month.

1 White Birds of the Sea and Shore

2 Greyheaded Gull

Larus cirrocephalus
R315

Similar birds
Hartlaub's Gull
R316

A score of these smallish gulls could be present at your first introduction. The Greyheaded Gull is a gregarious bird. Delicate greys blend with white to give a pristine image which is further enhanced by red bill and feet. Flight seems effortless with black wing-tips prominent.

You may be surprised to see your holiday gulls back home inland, perhaps circling the morning traffic. This is not unusual, as the Greyheaded Gull is not averse to fresh water – especially when there is a rubbish dump around for extra food. Muddy pools on an excavated construction site have on occasion attracted this immaculate little gull.

Breeding takes place in rowdy colonies on islands and in other sheltered places. Ground-level nests are simply constructed from grass and small sticks to hold two to three beautifully blotched eggs.

1 White Birds of the Sea and Shore

3 Cape Gannet
Morus capensis
R53

Similar birds
None

This predominantly white, large sea bird you probably will only meet while it is flying in a large flock offshore; that is, unless you visit one of the breeding islands. The striking black mask and throat stripe complement the yellow head to give a facial expression which can only be worn by a gannet.

When seriously fishing a substantial shoal, gannets change into missiles and dive deep into the sea, with wings partly folded and neck outstretched. Again and again they plunge, sometimes a hundred birds or more, to take mackerel, pilchard and other small fish from the deep green of the sea.

The Cape Gannet breeds off the South African coast on bird 'islands' and contributes to the guano deposits used as fertiliser. The dense colonies of breeding birds raise hollow-topped mounds and then humbly lay a single white egg in each.

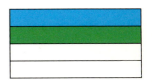

1 White Birds of the Sea and Shore

4 Dabchick

*Tachybaptus
ruficollis*
R8

Similar birds
Southern Pochard
R113

Your acquaintance with these small birds will be made while you're at the water's edge, as the dabchick fussily swims hither and thither like a mechanical toy, disappearing periodically beneath the surface as if someone had pulled a string.

Strangely lobed feet are attached to legs placed too far back to promote walking – swimming and diving are a speciality. Lack of a tail is part of the dabchick scene.

Frogs, from tadpole stage onwards, are the main fare in dabchick diets. That is what all the diving is about.

A waterlogged raft of water weeds is moored in among reeds or branches away from the bank, to serve as a nest. Plain white eggs, three or four of them, are tidily covered with weeds by the parents on leaving the nest. Diminutive dabchicks are piggy-backed until independent.

2 Divers of Inland Waters

5 Reed Cormorant

Phalacrocorax africanus
R58

Similar birds
Darter R60

Reed Cormorants are often seen swimming low in the water of a dam or pond, but look out for a bird sitting with wings outspread. If its bill is hooked at the tip and its eye is like a ruby, it is a Reed Cormorant. In response to a sudden invasion of its domain it will silently leave, flying arrowlike with quick wing-beats over the water.

Cormorants are divers and pursue both frogs and fish underwater, using their strong webbed feet while steering with their long, stiff tails. Cormorant plumage must be hung out to dry during the day to avoid waterlogging.

The Reed Cormorant seeks the company of other cormorants when roosting at night or breeding. A platform of sticks and similar material is put together for a nest, and two to five eggs are laid. Baby cormorants must be looked after for about a month before they are able to leave the nest.

2 Divers of Inland Waters

6 Redknobbed Coot

Fulica cristata
R228

Similar birds
Moorhen R226

There is a kind of domesticity about the coot you usually meet, with its characteristic call and fussy ways, a twig or weed in its beak. These birds sometimes gather in large flocks and run across the water as numerous disputes are declared and settled.

The Redknobbed Coot has a rounded plumpness as it potters in the water or walks about on land on longish legs and unwebbed feet. In the breeding season the two ripe-cherry knobs are prominent above the plastic white of the shield on the front of the head.

The coot is a committed vegetarian most of the time and food is taken as it comes: under the water, on the surface or even on land.

The coot makes a floating vegetable-matter nest. Lavish with its laying, mother coot ensures that six or more chicks take to water after hatching.

2 Divers of Inland Waters

7 Grey Heron

Ardea cinerea
R62

Similar birds
Purple Heron R65
Blackheaded Heron R63

Your meeting will be formal and any attempt to change this will result in the smoky grey, long-necked bird shedding its elegance and taking off clumsily. Once airborne, flight resumes a leisurely pace with neck retracted and long, yellowish legs trailing. This big bird often sits crone-like, neck withdrawn and one leg raised as if seeking a walking-stick.

It is a traditional bird and does most of its feeding in water, where frogs and fish are ready prey. Note the tall figure of heron locked in mid-stride knee-deep in water, waiting statuelike for an impatient frog to make the opening move.

At home in the heronry with others, the Grey Heron is a coarse, vulgar bird. Raucous and messy, it totters about on boughs too thin. A ragged nest of sticks holds two or three eggs which give rise to awkward baby herons with a poverty-stricken look.

3 Long-necked Stalkers of Veld and Vlei

8 Blackheaded Heron

Ardea melanocephala
R63

Similar birds
Purple Heron R65
Grey Heron R62

A tall figure of a big heron way out of bounds may be your first impression of the Blackheaded Heron. Your initial meeting may take place against the stark blackness of newly burnt veld, where this heron is hunting mice rather than frogs.

The Blackheaded Heron is chic compared to the Grey Heron, with a richness in the smart black trim on head and neck, set off by white of the throat and front. The long bill is in matching black. In flight the undersides of the wings show similar contrast.

This heron is more commonly associated with the open veld away from water, but is equally at home in a vlei.

The Blackheaded Heron roosts and breeds in heronries with other herons; it is no better behaved, in spite of its more formal appearance. Nest and eggs are similar to that of the Grey Heron.

3 Long-necked Stalkers of Veld and Vlei

9 Cattle Egret

Bubulcus ibis
R71

Similar birds
Little Egret R67
Yellowbilled Egret R68

You cannot meet cattle without meeting Cattle Egrets – there is a kind of partnership with all the benefits on the bird's side. Hairy buff plumage on head, neck and back separate the Cattle Egret from more elegant white relatives. Cattle Egrets flying to roost form long skeins to proclaim the end of the day.

Cattle Egrets are really herons which have forsaken water as a source of food. Instead they follow large animals to catch the insects in the grass which are disturbed by the movement. The name 'Tick Bird' is incorrect because the birds do not feed from the animals themselves.

It is only in the breeding and roosting places that the Cattle Egret acknowledges its heron heritage. It breeds in colonies and knocks together a stick platform in which it lays pale bluish eggs. Hairy egret chicks stagger about the branches after leaving the nest, until they are ready to fly.

3 Long-necked Stalkers of Veld and Vlei

10 Hamerkop
Scopus umbretta
R81

Similar birds
Hadeda Ibis R94

A sudden loss of goldfish could herald your first meeting with the Hamerkop. The dark bird which awkwardly flies up at your approach seems embarrassed at being found out. The hammerhead image will be appreciated even if the loss of fish is not.

Hamerkops potter in the water and mud on the fringes of pools and dams seeking a variety of small water animals. Occasionally they may stir the mud with their feet to get things moving.

Programmed by instinct the Hamerkop must build a nest bigger than every other bird's nest. The huge oven-like structure is put together in a substantial tree or on a cliff. It represents several wheelbarrow loads of sticks and other bits and pieces. The entrance tunnel is plastered with mud. Four or five white eggs are laid within and incubated by the parents until grey downy chicks emerge.

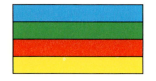

4 The Brown Enigma

11 White Stork

Ciconia ciconia
R83

Similar birds
Yellowbilled Stork
R90

The White Stork's fairy-tale image seems incongruous in our summer grassland scenario, but will nevertheless help you recognise this dignified bird of international fame. It is taller than most other birds of the open veld, and the white plumage with black wing-trim is distinctive. A red bill completes the picture. White Storks fly with their necks extended, soaring in great numbers on thermals at times, especially just before migration.

Locusts, a plague to man, are food to storks. Insecticide sprays directed against the locusts inevitably affect the birds which feed upon these insects.

The White Stork breeds in Europe (where the fairy-tales began) on special roof-top platforms. A few White Storks have regularly shirked the long journey north and instead breed in trees in the southern Cape.

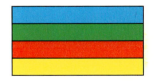

5 *Big-billed Striders*

12 Abdim's Stork

Ciconia abdimii
R85

Similar birds
Black Stork R84

A summer rugby field full of big, shiny black birds with white bellies may be your first introduction to Abdim's Stork. Go a little closer to confirm your identification, and big black wings will lift the birds after a short run. Having gained height, they soar themselves away into the distance. If the meetings grow to be more intimate, you may see a blue face with red trim behind a long, grey bill.

Slow deliberate strides carry Abdim's Stork over the open grassland. Insects, rodents and the odd reptile are picked up in passing. It is a kind of regimented mopping up operation.

These storks gather as if to ponder at watering-places and then fly off to roost in huge numbers in big gum trees or similar. Abdim's Storks leave us at the end of summer and head for Equatorial regions to breed.

5 Big-billed Striders

13 Blue Crane

Anthropoides paradisea
R208

Similar birds
Wattled Crane
R207
Grey Heron R62

Like graceful china ornaments, large groups of Blue Cranes gather in the veld, vlei or on cultivated lands, where you may meet them on your travels. Watch a little longer and you may see an elaborate spread-winged dance which is both beautiful and strange.

Blue Cranes soar to great heights with necks extended and call to each other in a loud, never-to-be-forgotten Blue Crane call.

The typical open-veld menu is enjoyed by cranes with new, green grain shoots added, to displease farmers. Frogs and fish may be included when feeding in vleis.

Camouflaged eggs are laid two to three in a clutch in an informal ground-level scrape with minor embellishment. Chicks are mobile almost immediately after hatching.

5 Big-billed Striders

14 Sacred Ibis
Threskiornis aethiopicus
R91

Similar birds
None

A massive V of big white birds gliding and flapping to roost is the memorable first meeting with the Sacred Ibis. Black heads, long bills and big white wings with mourning trim are impressions that will linger. On the ground the bird is somewhat different: neck, head and bill seem to be fabricated from an inferior black plastic material without feathers. A dull white body sports black plumes like chimney-sweeps' brushes stuck in as an afterthought.

The long, curved beak is made for probing mudflats, rubbish dumps, sewage ponds, manure heaps as potential sources of food. Groups of birds usually probe and pose throughout the day.

The Sacred Ibis breeds in colonies in guano-washed trees or even on the ground. Two or three whitish eggs are laid on a platform of sticks. Baby ibises have their plastic heads decently covered in down.

5 Big-billed Striders

15 Hadeda Ibis

Bostrychia hagedash
R94

Similar birds
Hamerkop R81
Glossy Ibis R93

An unforgettable, loud, cheap plastic-trumpet cry, as much part of the African scene as that of the Fish Eagle, informs you that you and one or more Hadeda have met. A big dark bird with wings which appear to be attached too far back, flaps over the trees in a 'sitting' position with beak facing down in a challenge to aerodynamic principles.

A more gentle introduction occurs when the birds are unaware of your presence, as they flap their way along a stream, calling to greet the day or bid it farewell, perhaps.

In the sunlight the purple iridescence on the shoulders gleams as if newly polished, and the bill shows its reddish tinge.

The Hadeda Ibis chooses to nest alone in a high river-bank tree. A frail platform of twigs is built to hold two to four heavily marked olive green eggs.

5 Big-billed Striders

16 Greater Flamingo

Phoenicopterus ruber
R96

Similar birds
Lesser Flamingo
R97

It will be a very formal meeting with a degree of awe, as hundreds, perhaps thousands of birds crystallise into graceful statues from fast-moving formations of scarlet wings. It is a privilege to see and appreciate this beautiful bird which does not seem to slot into tidy scientific classifications quite as easily as most.

The Greater Flamingo is more white than pink. It is a big bird with long, long red legs and a matching long neck to get back to ground level for feeding. Filtering devices strain off organisms as the bird feeds with beak inverted in shallow, brackish water.

Nests are tidy mounds of mud, hollow at the top to take a solitary egg. Hatching young must leave the nest and take to water after about five days to join flamingo nurseries.

6 Filter-feeders on Stilts

17 Egyptian Goose

Alopochen aegyptiacus
R102

Similar birds
South African
Shelduck R103

The Egyptian Goose is the one goose you are sure to meet; is is very widespread. Pinioned birds in parks mingle with wild birds and one doesn't know which is which. Almost every pan or dam has Egyptian Geese, and even suburban streams can support a pair or more. In flight this goose is magnificent. Wings white and black with dark green trailing trim, lift the heavy goose into strong flight.

The Egyptian Goose lives off grass and other vegetation, showing a liking for newly emerging wheat. It usually goes out morning and evening to feed, and lounges about in between.

Nests are established anywhere, from ground level to high in trees, on church steeples and on cliffs, and often far from water. The problems of getting six or more flightless young to water are mind-boggling.

7 Water-loving Game Birds

18 Yellow-billed Duck

Anas undulata
R104

Similar birds
Redbilled Teal
R108
Black Duck R105

A duck in classic duck-design is the Yellowbilled Duck; even to the domestic quack uttered by the females. The meeting-place could be any fair-sized expanse of fresh water with enough vegetation to provide food and shelter. The characteristic yellow beak is almost synthetic in its precision finish, and feathers covering dense down are smooth and neatly scaled. A glossy green speculum with white border adorns each wing.

The Yellowbilled Duck nibbles water plants in the shallows and turns tail up when the water is deeper. Grazing on land is also acceptable when the pickings are good.

This duck forms its nest in vegetation near water, then lines it with down to take up to a dozen cream-coloured eggs. Ducklings take to water after hatching.

7 Water-loving Game Birds

19 Secretary Bird

Sagittarius serpentarius
R118

Similar birds
Wattled Crane R207
Blue Crane R208

Your first encounter with a Secretary Bird will probably be from your car on its territory in a game reserve. One, perhaps two big, grey birds come strutting through the grass. Closer inspection will show long legs in black knickerbockers. An orange face, black crest and wing trim, and extended tail complete the diagnosis.

The Secretary Bird is unique to Africa south of the Sahara, and is designed to stride to catch its prey, which consists of almost anything: eggs, rodents, reptiles and even insects.

The flat-top acacia thorn-trees are made for Secretary Bird nests. It is on top of these trees that the big, flat platform of sticks which characterises the Secretary Bird's nest is placed. Two pale eggs are laid, usually in the summer months. Nearly four months must pass before the young will fly.

8 An Eagle on Foot

20 Cape Vulture

Gyps coprotheres
R122

Similar birds
Whitebacked Vulture R123

This will be a classic, one-sided meeting, with you the viewer a mere upward-looking speck in the panorama visible to the Cape Vulture, as it soars effortlessly on its daily food-patrol. Unless at a nest, or at a carcass, vulture meetings are usually with the bird in flight. The small, naked head, almost an afterthought in relation to huge wings, distinguishes the flying vulture from eagles.

The Cape Vulture feeds on carrion, tearing the flesh from the bones with its powerful beak. Where the carcass is big and enthusiasm great, the bickering birds become covered in blood. Bone fragments are part of the diet; and must form part of the nestling's diet too, if a healthy vulture is to ensue.

High on the guano-white cliff face, the Cape Vultures nest in colonies. A few twigs and a rocky ledge must hold the single egg for two months and the flightless nestling for another three months.

9 Hunters from the Sky

21 Black-shouldered Kite

Elanus caeruleus
R127

Similar birds
None

You can meet at least one Blackshouldered Kite a day, often within the city boundaries. Grassy freeway verges breed rodents, and it is not uncommon to see a Blackshouldered Kite above the traffic in the early morning. A few birds become casualties before they learn to recognise the hazard of cars in the heat of the chase. This small raptor is a beautiful blend of blue-grey, white and black with yellow accessories.

Small rodents are top of the diet list. Using a hovering technique, the kite expertly lowers itself for the kill. Outstretched claws take the prey in a final drop.

The Blackshouldered Kite builds a twiggy platform on top of a tree and lines it with grass to form its nest. Three or four spotted buff eggs are laid in spring or autumn on the highveld. Like many raptors, the immature birds must endure a drab-brown spell.

9 Hunters from the Sky

22 Black Eagle
Aquila verreauxii
R131

Similar birds
Wahlberg's Eagle
R135

Most meetings will be from below, with this truly great eagle soaring above you. White 'windows' in the broad-tip, black wings confirm identity. To see a flying Black Eagle from above is to experience the vastness of this bird's domain. The white V on the back, and yellow face and feet are the only features which relieve the sombre black plumage.

The Black Eagle lives mainly from dassies snatched from their rocky look-out points in passing. Game birds, hares and small buck are also fair game at times. Chickens and lambs are only rarely taken.

The Black Eagle builds a nest on sheer kranses, in which two white eggs, sometimes marked, are laid. However, nature decrees that the older chick must kill the younger for the species to survive; so only one young bird will leave the nest, three months after hatching. It takes a long time to make one more Black Eagle.

9 Hunters from the Sky

23 African Fish Eagle

Haliaeetus vocifer
R148

Similar birds
Whiteheaded
Vulture R125

The call of the Fish Eagle is Africa's copyright. Uttered with head flung back to await the echo, this wild cry is heard across rivers, lakes, lagoons and estuaries many, many times at the start of each day. The gleaming white head contrasting sharply with the chestnut and black of the body form lasting memories of the Fish Eagle in its water-based domain.

This eagle is not always a noble hunting bird; it will eat dead fish, nestlings and eggs of other waterbirds. However, it is able to stoop to take living fish from the water.

Trees both living and dead are used to support a huge stick-nest, where height rather than concealment is relied upon to protect the eggs and young. Two eggs are laid in the winter months and around forty-five days later eaglets hatch. Another two and a half months of patient feeding is necessary before the young eagles leave the nest.

9 Hunters from the Sky

24 Coqui Francolin

Francolinus coqui
R188

Similar birds
Shelley's Francolin
R191
Orange River
Francolin R193

It could be a group meeting, with several of these small francolins 'freezing' in the grass to avoid detection. Such evasive tactics practised on open roads in the face of traffic, have disastrous consequences and ruin an introduction.

The male and female Coqui Francolin each have distinctive plumage, but both are exquisitely marked in bars, streaks and stripes of mingled buff, brown and yellow.

This francolin is a member of the widespread pheasant and partridge family and lives off seeds, green shoots, and insects, including ticks.

A shrub or grass-tussock provides the necessary cover for a ground-level nest which is little more than a grass-lined hollow. About five white to off-white eggs are laid in summer. Tiny, clockwork chicks are mobile soon after hatching, but like many small things they must learn to run before they fly.

10 Ground-loving Wildfowl

25 Swainson's Francolin

Francolinus swainsonii
R199

Similar birds
Natal Francolin
R196

Your first acquaintance will probably be with one or more of these birds running indecently fast with head held low. Running birds may suddenly take flight over a short distance and then sprint off again. A more leisurely study of this wary Francolin shows the bare, red skin of the face and throat which contrasts sharply with dull camouflage plumage.

The Swainson's Francolin has adjusted to the replacement of grass and bush with cultivation, and no doubt supplements its diet of seeds, fruits and bulbs with the easy pickings of man.

Like other francolins the Swainson's Francolin lays its eggs in a simple nest hidden in the grass. Up to a dozen off-white eggs make up the clutch. Young francolins are mobile immediately after hatching and move like mottled, mechanical toys in the undergrowth, supervised and protected by the parent birds.

10 Ground-loving Wildfowl

26 Helmeted Guineafowl

Numida meleagris
R203

Similar birds
Crested Guinea-Fowl R204

The Guineafowl on the fringes of the city have become urbanised rather than give way to township development. Rounded, graphite-grey birds rendered more visible by the burning of grass are now often seen on open plots. In the morning light they look like cannon-balls.

Monotonous whistling mingled with grating alarm calls has added to the city's repertoire of sounds.

Like domestic fowls they scratch food and eat almost anything. When alarmed they run with affronted dignity and often fly high for short distances. They sometimes perch uncomfortably on high-level power lines.

The large flocks break up into pairs for breeding in midsummer. Up to twenty eggs may be laid in a hollow lined with grass. Parents trail chicks until they are able to fly; then parents with their young again form flocks.

10 Ground-loving Wildfowl

27 Black Korhaan

Eupodotis afra
R239

Similar birds
Redcrested Korhaan R237

An audacious male Black Korhaan shrieks his indignation at you for even contemplating a meeting on korhaan territory; while his mate quietly slips away as if not properly dressed for receiving visitors. The male is assertive, noisy and a dandy to boot, given to flaunting his black-and-white image from the tops of anthills and also in flight.

Both sexes are cleverly camouflaged from above when their tweedy brown plumage on the back and wings merges into their grassy habitat. Look for the bright yellow legs to help you confirm that the korhaan you have met is in fact the Black Korhaan.

The female is committed to incubate the one or two heavily marked eggs while the male aids and abets the deception techniques used to lead you away from the nest or chicks.

10 Ground-loving Wildfowl

28 Three-banded Plover

Charadrius tricollaris
R249

Similar birds
Kittlitz's Plover
R248

This little plover courses the water-line in tiny-legged sprints, stopping to bob and survey the scene as you approach. When the meeting starts to become too threatening the bird flies off quickly, low over the water to settle further on. Each take-off is accompanied by a shrill one- or two-syllable call. Three bands on the chest, two of black and one of white, identify this plover. A neutral, warm grey back blends with the pastel shades of the shore.

Feeding is a mud-probing exercise yielding the insects and small crustaceans which keep these small birds in trim.

Two pebbly eggs are laid in a 'pebble-dashed' hollow near the water. With care these hatch into minute plover chicks which also sprint along the shore in cryptic fuzz until enough feathers come to support flight.

11 Runners on Dry Land and Wet

29 Crowned Plover

Vanellus coronatus
R255

Similar birds
Wattled Plover
R260

The Crowned Plover has so invaded the domain of man that meetings are no longer optional. It seems as though these plovers need regular encounters with man and his pets as an excuse to shriek abuse. They crowd the grassy verges of highways and interchanges; they invade sports fields and smallholdings; their distribution grows as they thrive on the protection of man and motor car.

These birds perform a valuable service as they patrol the veld on long, red legs; for between their bouts of aggression, they eat pests such as harvester termites, locusts and caterpillars.

When nesting, the heckling and harassing behaviour reaches an all-time high. Staggering around in a hemiplegic broken-wing act to lead you away from eggs and young is alternated with daring dive-bombing activity. Eggs and young are marked to merge with the habitat.

11 Runners on Dry Land and Wet

30 Spotted Dikkop

Burhinus capensis
R297

Similar birds
Water Dikkop
R298

The Spotted Dikkop is a furtive bird skulking in the shadows with lowered head as though it has something to hide. At dusk the scene changes and they emerge to feed and pipe to the moon. The dikkop is something like a plover in another garb; plumage on the back is heavily spotted dark chocolate on a pale caramel base. Large, yellow eyes question your approach, and a yellow leg is lifted in anticipation of retreat.

The dikkop feeds at night, sometimes in suburban gardens, on a mixed diet of insects and grass seeds, with the occasional frog thrown in.

Breeding is a ritual which puts these birds into a highly excitable and aggressive state. When nest or young are approached, horses and other large animals are dive-bombed without discretion. This is understandable if one considers how easily camouflaged eggs laid on the bare ground could be trodden on.

11 Runners on Dry Land and Wet

31 Rock Pigeon

Columba guinea
R349

Similar birds
Feral Pigeon R348
Rameron Pigeon R350

The Rock Pigeon is a wild bird of the kranses and koppies which has taken civilisation too seriously. Your meeting with this pigeon which has moved into towns and cities is casual, and almost taken for granted. This richly coloured bird with fine white speckles and characteristic red eyepatch is very familiar.

The Rock Pigeon flies in flocks from the built-up areas to feed on grain and other foods subsidised by the farmers. It returns at night to roost and adorn buildings with its white droppings.

Breeding is a year-round affair. The male pigeons display their prowess by cooing urgently and beating their wings together between glides. An austere platform of twigs and grass is the traditional nest, but city types may even use pieces of wire as a bed for their two white eggs.

Ubiquitous Birds that Coo

32 Cape Turtle Dove

Streptopelia capicola
R354

Similar birds
Redeyed Dove
R352

The Cape Turtle Dove is probably the second most common dove in our region. It is a regular contributor to the sounds of Africa, where its call provokes nostalgia. Your first introduction to this dove may be as it flies steeply upwards 'towering' from a tree, then glides down again with grating call uttered on landing to proclaim a territory. Soft dove-grey plumage in varying shades promotes the olive-branch image of peace. It wears a black collar backwards on its neck.

Later you will meet the same bird on the ground, walking as though head and legs were linked to bob and tread in unison. Seeds and insects are picked up with midwalk pauses, during these ground feeding spells. Twigs and rootlets are arranged in a typical dove nesting-platform secured to the fork of a tree. Building is a joint enterprise between male and female and so is incubation.

12 Ubiquitous Birds that Coo

33 Laughing Dove

Streptopelia senegalensis
R355

Similar birds
Greenspotted Dove R358

Almost anywhere you go there has to be a Laughing Dove that got there first. In the city centre or in the bush, or even in the open veld, these birds will be seen foraging on the ground or lining up to drink where water is available. Traditional dove-grey is suffused with pink in the colour scheme of this bird. A black spotted design worn on the chest, and upper plumage of pale slate blue mingled with cinnamon, are Laughing Dove trade marks.

This dove also eats grain like other doves, but it is quite prepared to join the flying-termite feast which occurs after rain and attracts a host of wild creatures.

The Laughing Dove is a highly successful species, turning out a new generation of doves several times per year without changing the nesting site.

12 Ubiquitous Birds that Coo

34 Grey Lourie

Corythaixoides concolor
R373

Similar birds
Purplecrested Lourie R371

You will meet this bird in drier parts of the country and even on the fringes of highveld cities during drought years. In flight it is big and gawky, landing on a branch as though it came up sooner than expected. Its mechanical bounding about a tree is inelegant but very efficient. The loud, extended 'go-'way' call uttered as you come too close, will never be forgotten.

The Grey Lourie is the plain relative in a family of birds regularly feathered in gorgeous greens, intense blues and purples, and deep crimson. The traditional lourie diet of fruit is supplemented with the specialities of the bush environment.

A frugal platform-nest is prescribed by instinct for all louries, and Grey Louries usually place theirs in thorn-trees. A relative may be called in to help when white eggs turn to chicks.

13 Tree-bound Curiosities

35 Redchested Cuckoo

Cuculus solitarius
R377

Similar birds
European Cuckoo
R374

'Piet-my-vrou', the characteristic early summer call of the Redchested Cuckoo, echoes from a tall tree; prompting a meeting perhaps. Patient investigation shows a bird with a reddish chest and a barred underside well hidden high in the tree. You are more likely to encounter the fledged chick cheeping urgently for food from frantic host parents which are programmed by instinct to feed their unplanned foster child. The barred chest and belly proclaim the cuckoo heritage of the baby.

Cuckoos have a weakness for caterpillars and time their visit to us to coincide with the hatching of these and the breeding of suitable host bird species. In winter the cuckoos and their ill-gotten offspring migrate northwards.

Parasitism is family planning at its best, where a mate, a host and a date must be found and co-ordinated with great accuracy.

14 Traditional Parasites and Relatives

36 Diederik Cuckoo

Chrysococcyx caprius
R386

Similar birds
Klaas's Cuckoo
R385

Shimmering bronzy-green with white accessories is a simple description of the Diederik Cuckoo which you can easily meet during any summer in your own garden. These cuckoos are the high-pressure parasites that plague weaver colonies. You may also meet a glossy youngster pleading malnutrition while anxious foster parents force food past the ever-open red bill.

The Diederik Cuckoo's repetitive call is like its name, with a tone of lament. It is part of the summertime season of bird-calls in southern Africa. This cuckoo too leaves at the end of summer for warmer parts of Africa.

Only one egg is laid in the host's nest to replace the one eaten by the female cuckoo; this must match the remaining eggs and be timed to hatch while the host's young are small enough to be evicted.

14 Traditional Parasites and Relatives

37 Burchell's Coucal

Centropus superciliosus R391

Similar birds
Green Coucal
R387

Coucals are undercover birds favouring thickets and are usually only seen when they break cover to fly across a road. The rusty wings, heavy black head and tail contrast with creamy underside and make identification of the Burchell's Coucal quite easy for those who are eager to meet one. The coucal is a relative of the cuckoo but honour in the nesting place is observed and baby coucals are raised by their parents.

The Burchell's Coucal is a predatory bird which extends its insect diet to include baby birds. In a suburban garden a resident coucal is not always welcome for this reason.

Within its thicket territory this coucal puts together a big, ball-shaped bundle of dry vegetation which is hollow inside, to use as a nest. Four or so white eggs are laid to ensure a fair contribution to the future coucal population.

14 Traditional Parasites and Relatives

38 Barn Owl
Tyto alba
R392

Similar birds
Grass Owl R393

This is the owl of steeples, caves, outbuildings and old mine-shafts, whose ghostly whiteness and silent flight have made the superstitious tremble. Dark eyes, set like beads into a long, heart-shaped, unbirdlike face have further stimulated the imagination.

If an acquaintance should grow, you will get to know a most beautiful bird. Upper parts are a fashion-fabric blend of yellow ochre overlaid with patterned grey; breast and belly are snowy white with discreet spotting. Legs appear in long white drawers, to mask their true function of plucking rodents and birds from life.

Breeding is a staggered affair where the first egg may be near to hatching before the last egg of the half-dozen or more is laid. Ledges and hollows are nesting sites of choice, where owlets are safe while parents hunt to feed a demanding brood.

15 Night-time Hunters and Associates

39 Pearl-spotted Owl

Glaucidium perlatum
R398

Similar birds
Scops Owl R396

This is a small owl of the daytime and the night, with a preference for the bushveld. Bulbuls could make the noisy introduction in your first meeting with a Pearlspotted Owl, and it will only be the round, owly eyes and face-pattern that will enable you to separate the owl from the birds mobbing it.

When you hear the characteristic loud whistling call of this owl, perhaps duetting with a mate, follow the bulbuls' excited calls; it could lead to a rendezvous with a special little bird. Mice, small reptiles, frogs and birds as big as the owl itself, are all on the 'hit-list' when it comes to feeding.

Last year's barbet nest-holes are where the Pearlspotted Owl lays its clutch of white eggs, which eventually produce two or three fat little owls which seem bigger than the parent birds feeding them.

15 *Night-time Hunters and Associates*

40 Spotted Eagle Owl

Bubo africanus
R401

Similar birds
Cape Eagle Owl
R400

The first meeting could well be on the road after dark, when a big greyish bird takes flight, briefly catching the car lights before melting into the night. Subsequent encounters may be with an eared silhouette on top of a pole at dusk. Only an intimate meeting will reveal the true character of this big owl.

Warmly-clad in granny-print plumage, the Spotted Eagle Owl is a killing machine to small rodents. Legs in knitted stockings end in powerful claws which penetrate and crush the prey. Yet this is quite a timid bird, which hisses and claps its beak when afraid.

Baby eagle owls come into a world which may be no more than a rock overhang, or at best a second-hand nest from some other bird. Covered in austerity-grade fluff the owlets which hatch at ground level soon move away from the nest to blend with the veld.

15 Night-time Hunters and Associates

41 Fierynecked Nightjar

Caprimulgus pectoralis
R405

Similar birds
European Nightjar
R404
Freckled Nightjar
R408

Suddenly there is a legless, birdlike creature with big eyes, glued to the farm road in front of the car, mesmerised it would seem by the headlights. Unwittingly you have met a nightjar. Go a little closer and the shape unglues itself with a flash of white-spotted wings and tail before it vanishes into the darkness.

The nightjar is a highly specialised bird of the night with a huge mouth fringed with bristles for scooping insects from the air as it silently flies. The shades and shadows of dried leaves and rough bark are caught up in the plumage of the nightjar to ensure an almost perfect blend with its habitat.

The Fierynecked Nightjar's characteristic call is unmistakable. It can be enjoyed even though you may never see how baby nightjars are reared in a dead-leaf nest upon the ground.

15 Night-time Hunters and Associates

42 Whiterumped Swift

Apus caffer
R415

Similar birds
Little Swift R417
Horus Swift R416

Swifts are confusingly similar, but quite distinct from swallows with which they are sometimes muddled. Built to fly they are almost constantly in flight, even mating at high altitude. Your introduction to the Whiterumped Swift will be a fleeting affair when a fast-flying bird whips by with barely a glimpse of white.

The Whiterumped Swift is a smallish, streamlined bird with a wide, insect-catching gape behind a tiny beak, and little gripping claws for legs. Powerful sickle-shaped wings dominate a body which holds everything together. Nondescript but neat dark plumage is a swift feature.

The Whiterumped Swift nests in crevices or in appropriated nests of swallows. It observes swift tradition by gluing feathers together with saliva to make a bed for its white eggs. Young get only one chance to show they can fly.

16 Crescent-winged Fliers and Similar

43 European Swallow

Hirundo rustica
R518

Similar birds
Whitethroated Swallow R520

The European Swallow imports itself by the millions into southern Africa each summer from the temperate regions of the Northern Hemisphere. At the end of the season they gather once again and fly back to familiar nesting sites as far afield as Russia. Reddish forehead and throat, white breast with gun-blue uppers and classic swallow tail, are typical.

These story-book swallows come here to feast upon our summer; tons of flying insects must be consumed during their stay. At sunset they gather in thousands to roost in reed-bed retreats.

April comes and migration messages are exchanged in urgent twitterings. Then you will see the European Swallows as they perch upon the multiple overhead wires between the poles – like written music notes in what we may in fantasy perceive as the swan-song of summer.

16 Crescent-winged Fliers and Similar

44 Lesser Striped Swallow

Hirundo abyssinica
R527

Similar birds
Greater Striped
Swallow R526

Once the formalities of that first meeting are over and your house or shed has passed the building-site test, you can look forward to an early-spring rendezvous with Lesser Striped Swallows for years to come. These small, wispy swallows about your home are a joy, even though a nest of mud beneath the eaves results. Densely striped white breast, russet trim on head and rump, and the blue-black sheen on back and wings identify the Lesser Striped Swallow.

Food is taken in flight that seems joyful and free. When feeding is over the birds perch and continue their gentle untuned song, begun in flight.

Tiny beakfuls of mud make up the bowl-and-tunnel nest and the timely arrival of rain or man-made substitute is a key factor in this swallow's breeding programme. Each year a new nest is built; last year's model is left for swifts and sparrows.

16 Crescent-winged Fliers and Similar

45 Speckled Mousebird

Colius striatus
R424

Similar birds
Whitebacked Mousebird R425
Redfaced Mousebird R426

This long-tailed bird of Africa is likely to be one of your earlier introductions to bird-life, especially if you are a gardener. Set aside the wrath for a moment and watch; the Speckled Mousebird is a gentle pest. Hanging from the branches with feet at eye-level, clambering about within thick foliage, or flying in a small flock, it is easy to see how these birds earned their name. Sleeping is done in bunches, with heads in a huddle and tails left to hang. Nondescript grey-brown plumage, with fine barring, distinguishes the Speckled Mousebird from its more striking relatives.

Fruit is the main fare, but flowers and seedlings are added to a diet that does not win friends.

The mousebird nest is a second-rate structure where tidiness is not the theme. A lined bowl within holds up to four creamy-white eggs.

17 Mouse-like Lovers of Fruit

46 Pied Kingfisher

Ceryle rudis
R428

Similar birds
None

It will be a leisure-time meeting with the Pied Kingfisher, for this bird conspicuously frequents these places. Fishing or boating on river, lake or estuary you can hardly fail to notice this long-beaked, boldly speckled, black and white bird, sitting on branch or wire. Suddenly the bird will rise high into the air and hover, beak down, and plan the next move. It could be a dive ending in a splash and a fish to show, or a nonchalant return to perch, as if to say it wasn't really big enough anyway.

Fish swallowed whole are this fisher's food. To ensure a smooth passage down an elastic gullet, the prey is beaten into immobility against a branch or stone.

Baby Pied Kingfishers emerge from eggs into a world of darkness, in a hollow at the end of a burrow longer than your arm. There they stay until able to fly.

18 Fishers Genuine and Modified

47 Malachite Kingfisher

Alcedo cristata
R431

Similar birds
Pygmy Kingfisher
R432

It has to be a fleeting encounter, for the Malachite Kingfisher is not one to wait as you blunder into its secluded, waterside domain. However, should one stray to your pond, you may have a chance to observe this tiny, jewel-like bird at rest. The rich blue plumage of nape and back contrasts sharply with the warm orangy hue of breast and belly. Loosely laid malachite feathers on the head form a crest. Short legs end in tiny, plastic feet made to fit perches from which to fish. A long, sharp bill finished in red is made for fishing.

Small fish are high on the feeding priority list, but tadpoles, little frogs and water-borne insects are also fair game.

This fragile-looking bird faithfully observes kingfisher lore and burrows deeply into a bank to nest. As a gesture, the nesting chamber is lined with indigestible bits of fish.

18 Fishers Genuine and Modified

48 Brownhooded Kingfisher

Halcyon albiventris
R435

Similar birds
Striped Kingfisher
R437

This kingfisher is one of several which have abandoned fishing and have adopted a dry-land way of life. A meeting in a rural garden would not be unusual, for the Brownhooded Kingfisher makes its presence felt. Loud calls and an open-winged bob-hopping display cannot be ignored; even in retreat, this bird will draw your attention with the flash of brilliant blue on wings, back and tail. The long red beak, originally designed for effective capture of aquatic prey, has been retained in this land-locked version.

Lizards, scorpions and spiders make up a witches'-brew diet which may be further garnished with snakes, crabs and mice.

The Brownhooded Kingfisher drills a tunnel in a sandy bank, ending in a nesting chamber. Only a cunning snake or active rodent are any real threat to eggs or young.

18 Fishers Genuine and Modified

49 Little Bee-eater

Merops pusillus
R444

Similar birds
Whitefronted Bee-eater R443

The Little Bee-eater is a perfect miniature of a classic bee-eater. With upper plumage as green as the trees it frequents, the beautiful little bird often escapes from view. Catch a glimpse of lemon-yellow throat and deeper-yellow chest and belly, separated by a collar of black and a meeting must ensue. A long, sharp beak with a downward curve, which merges with the black eye-stripe is what all bee-eaters wear. Legs are small and not for walking so business is conducted from a perch.

Aided by a mate, equally gorgeous, these birds skilfully hawk flying insects from a favoured, thin-twig perch.

Although it seems so ill-equipped for excavation duties, the Little Bee-eater bores its nesting tunnel in any convenient sandy bank, perhaps only half a metre high.

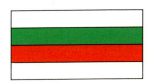

19 Elegant Hawkers of Bees and Kin

50 Lilac-breasted Roller

Coracias caudata
R447

Similar birds
Purple Roller R449

The Lilacbreasted Roller is not a modest bird, and brilliant blue plumage must be flaunted, whether at rest on a prominent perch, or in flight, rolling and looping to win a mate. This living blend of lilac and shades of blue is about as eye-catching as a bird can be. It is not a bird of the town and prefers the solitude of the bushveld scene without many fellow rollers about.

Rollers are well-equipped with a strong bill to go out and get the food they prefer. Scorpions, snakes, centipedes, caterpillars, locusts and even mice and birds are taken live on forays to the ground.

Rollers are hole-nesting birds but do not themselves make holes in trees; they must wait for Nature to do it for them, before they can lay their eggs. Unfortunately there is usually a tree-hole shortage in roller territory, and competition with other birds and mammals is keen.

20 Brilliant Blue Sentinels of the Bush

51 Hoopoe
Upupa epops
R451

Similar birds
None

The Hoopoe is the only member of a family that extends through Africa to Europe and then on through Asia to Japan. It is truly an international model. In design it is unique: no other bird in our country combines a long, slender bill, like a Stone Age sewing needle, with a Red Indian head-dress which can fold like a fan. The cinnamon of body and head forms a muted backdrop for wings which are boldly patterned in black and white.

The Hoopoe is a walking bird with short legs, so it takes on an air of urgency as it probes the lawn with its long beak for worms.

Nesting takes place in a natural or man-made hole in virtually anything from an anthill to a brick wall carelessly built. Nestlings start smelling foul soon after hatching in the unlined nest; a deterrent to predators, perhaps?

21 The Long Beak and Head-dress Theme

52 Redbilled Wood-hoopoe

Phoeniculus purpureus
R452

Similar birds
Scimitarbill R454

While the Redbilled Woodhoopoe is distantly related to the Hoopoe, they cannot even meet on common ground these days. The woodhoopoe is a rowdy, gregarious bird which lives its life in trees. Fitted with a long, bright red beak at one end and a long tail at the other, these woodhoopoes bow and bob to each other in a spontaneous ritual that makes your first contact memorable. In flight white trim on wings and tail is set off against the iridescent black of the rest of the bird.

Insects and other crawling creatures are the usual diet, with the odd gecko taken while probing bark for food. These woodhoopoes have been trespassing in the nest holes of other birds under suspicious circumstances.

Nesting is a tail-twisting business in a woodpecker hole or similar. One pair in the group does the breeding and the others help out with feeding.

21 The Long Beak and Head-dress Theme

53 Yellow-billed Hornbill

Tockus flavirostris
R459

Similar birds
Redbilled Hornbill
R458

If man had designed the Yellowbilled Hornbill some would consider it kitsch; but in nature this quaintly assembled bird is a pleasure to met. The big, yellow bill is not formidable and of lightweight construction. The eyes, set in pink skin, match the colour of the bill and contribute to a quizzical expression exclusive to hornbills. The bird itself presents a round-shouldered geriatric image, bordering on the scraggy side. A big tail, loosely fitted, is brought along as an afterthought.

Eating is mostly a ground-level exercise. Almost anything which moves and is not too big to swallow features in the diet of this bird.

Nesting is a conspiracy which leaves the female sealed in a hole in a tree, utterly dependent on her mate until the young hatch. When she breaks free the young reseal the nest until they are equipped to fly.

22 Bills, Bills and More Bills

54 Ground Hornbill

Bucorvus leadbeateri
R463

Similar birds
None

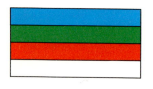

What prompted the creation of a hornbill as big as a turkey and then decreed that it should walk along the ground for most of its life, we shall never know. The Ground Hornbill is indeed the odd bird out in the family. The meeting-place will almost certainly be a bushveld game reserve when a big, black bird sporting bright red accoutrements strides into your life. There could be several more in the party. Notice the white wing-feathers as these huge, dark birds fly powerfully away.

This hornbill is strictly non-vegetarian. Insects are snacks; snakes, tortoises and even hares are main-course items.

Nesting calls for a big hole in a tree, but if not available a similar hole in a cliff is acceptable. Again this hornbill breaks with custom and does not seal up the nest. Instead a co-operative feeding scheme for brooding female and young is set up.

22 Bills, Bills and More Bills

55 Blackcollared Barbet

Lybius torquatus
R464

Similar birds
Pied Barbet R465

The Blackcollared Barbet could easily be a neighbour in many gardens in the eastern parts of the country. Listen for the loud duet as the first clue of the presence of these barbets, then look for a greenish bird carrying a red and black head too big for its body: a meeting is almost guaranteed. A well-stocked bird-table will also help to draw these birds from the trees. The powerful, black beak is useful for making holes in wood, and strong claws make clinging to vertical branches an easy task.

Fruit is the main food of barbets and should be included on bird-tables when barbets are about. In wilder places the indigenous figs are favoured.

Wood boring is a barbet speciality and this it must do to be able to breed. Where dead trees are in short supply, willow or sisal nesting-logs put up by bird gardeners are readily accepted.

23 Peckers of Wood and Beneficiaries

56 Crested Barbet

Trachyphonus vaillantii
R473

Similar birds
None

The Crested Barbet is a matey bird with a cottage-industry, patchwork look. It adopts gardens and readily accepts bird-table offerings. You may meet this untidy-looking bird while it is hopping along the ground, as if actuated by a spring that is too strong, or its tuneless early morning trill may drive you to find the perpetrator, and so provoke a less friendly encounter. Whatever the circumstances, you will soon recognise this bird. Feathers on the back and tail are black, patterned with white, and it wears a collar of black over a speckled, yellowish chest. A rakish crest completes the picture.

The Crested Barbet eats a variety of foods, as visits to the bird-table will show.

A nest is carved out of dead wood, preferably willow. In this hole three or more broods of baby barbets could emerge before the summer is out.

23 Peckers of Wood and Beneficiaries

57 Cardinal Woodpecker

Dendropicos fuscescens
R486

Similar birds
Bearded Woodpecker R487

The Cardinal Woodpecker is a traditional woodpecker, complete with red toupee in the male and a corresponding black one in the female. You will meet them in trees, usually together. Initially this clockwork tree climber will dodge behind a branch hoping you saw nothing. But be patient. Curiosity will bring it back into view. Strong claws enable woodpeckers to cling to branches in any position, using their stiffened tails like portable seats. The Cardinal Woodpecker is speckled and barred to blend with bark.

A chisel bill is used to make drumming noises, as well as to probe grubs from beneath bark and out of holes in dry wood.

Woodpeckers need dead wood in their lives, and their presence in your garden will depend on your tolerance of trees that are dead or partially so. Feeding and nest-hole construction depend on it.

58 Redthroated Wryneck

Jynx ruficollis
R489

Similar birds
Cardinal Woodpecker R486

The Redthroated Wryneck looks as though it was casually whittled from a strip of mottled grey bark. The rufous patch on throat and breast could easily have been pastelled in afterwards to embellish the carver's work. Vaguely similar to a woodpecker, the wryneck does not have a stiff tail and is not equipped to drill holes in wood. Harsh calling of the male and the female's enthusiastic reply, could prompt your first meeting with a bird that could otherwise pass unnoticed in your garden.

A diet of ants and termites brings the wryneck down to ground level to feed, where it awkwardly walks with legs and feet made for sitting in trees.

The wryneck is committed to nest in holes, with a preference for the cast-off nests of woodpeckers or barbets, as it cannot make its own. It could also breed in a well-designed artificial nest box.

23 Peckers of Wood and Beneficiaries

59 Rufousnaped Lark
Mirafra africana
R494

Similar birds
Sabota Lark R498

The Rufousnaped Lark has a habit of perching on a post, bush or anthill and singing in a sweet accompaniment to the muted sounds of wide-open spaces. Browns and buffs mingle with gentle markings on breast and back to merge with the grassland habitat. With its crest raised and chest out-thrust in song, your first impression of this small bird is one of an uninhibited wild creature in close communion with nature. Larks are confusingly similar in their manner and plumage. They are birds of wide open spaces and here you must go to find them.

Insects, spiders and other crawling creatures that share the lark's domain are the main source of food.

The nest is a cup of grass and rootlets with a domed roof, all intimately woven into the base of a grassy tussock. Here two or three small eggs, with spots and blotches to aid concealment, are laid.

60 Forktailed Drongo

Dicrurus adsimilis
R541

Similar birds
Black Flycatcher
R694

The meeting is often arranged, not by you, but by the Forktailed Drongoes who want to take advantage of the security afforded by human habitation. An aggressive pair of black birds with forked tails will enter your life and remain there while they raise their family. Cats and dogs will be cursed and dive-bombed regularly; crows, owls and passing hawks will be recklessly harassed in the air. Drongoes will mimic the calls of other birds and even the miaow of the cat, and intersperse these with their own rusty-hinge ramblings.

Posing as an insectivorous bird innocently taking insects in flight or on the ground, the drongo sometimes turns into a bird killer.

A drongo nest is an open-wove, twiggy cup bound with spider web, set high on an exposed branch. During a good season you may see a parent on eggs feeding a fat chick from the previous brood.

25 Aggressive Mimics of Farm and Garden

61 Blackheaded Oriole

Oriolus larvatus
R545

Similar birds
European Golden
Oriole R543

Mellifluous could have been the word coined to describe the orioles' whistling call, seemingly sweetened by the nectar upon which it feeds in winter. The Blackheaded Oriole is hasty and not given to waiting about while you arrange a meeting. A swiftly departing yellow bird, bigger than a weaver, is all you may see. Patience and a pair of binoculars will introduce you to a beautiful bird in shades of yellow, with a coal-black head, neck and breast, contrasting sharply with a coral beak. Black plumage is sometimes gilded with pollen from flowers explored for nectar. Big aloes with flowery racemes held high on candelabra stems draw this oriole from its tree-top domain to supplement, with nectar, a diet of insects. High in the trees it usually frequents, the Blackheaded Oriole assembles its cup nest from lichens and moss, then secures it with spider web to hang in a slender fork.

26   Golden Whistlers of Big-treed Gardens

62 Pied Crow
Corvus albus
R548

Similar birds
Black Crow R547

The Pied Crow is a twentieth-century scavenger geared to exploit the pickings of a technological age without forsaking its links with the rural world. You meet them everywhere: on highways prodding at a flattened cat; at rubbish dumps inspecting trash; in the veld looking for eggs and nestlings; and in the mountains waiting for something to sicken and die. Their rubbish removal role cannot be denied; their proliferation is regrettable as it can only be to the detriment of more sensitive species. The Pied Crow is an intelligent creature, swaggering as it walks as if with hands behind its back to improve the view of a white waistcoat.

A tall tree is a traditional nesting site, but these days power-line poles and windmills are acceptable. Modern nests may incorporate wire and other flotsam and jetsam of humans in a bowl big enough to hold four or five growing crows until they can fly.

27 Raucous Associates of Man

63 Arrow-marked Babbler

Turdoides jardineii
R560

Similar birds
Olive Thrush R577

Raucous consternation seems to be the bond that holds a group of Arrowmarked Babblers together in the bushy habitat they favour. A rural garden feeding-table with bone-meal on offer, is a good place to meet these noisy birds in the open. An indignant orange eye contrasts with the various shades of brown which dominate the plumage of the bird. The breast is liberally streaked with chalky arrowheads which lend a pattern to an otherwise plain-looking garb.

Insects and other crawling animals encountered during low-level scrounging in thickets, are the main food items, especially where no feeding scheme exists.

It is a case of 'all beaks in' when the gang gets down to nest-building with grass and twigs. Sitting on eggs and feeding young is also a communal affair.

28 Gregarious Noise-makers of the Thickets

64 Blackeyed Bulbul

Pycnonotus barbatus
R568

Similar birds
Redeyed Bulbul
R567
Cape Bulbul R566

The Blackeyed Bulbul and its relatives above, divide southern Africa between them in three separate territories fitting like the pieces of a jigsaw. They share a trade-mark patch of bright lemon secluded beneath the tail, and darkish heads with a gentle crest. Their separate identities are indelibly stencilled in the colour of the wattle round eye. You will encounter the blackeyed version in eastern parts of the country. Urgent calling in response to cat, snake or owl sets off a chain reaction involving other birds, and you if you are interested.

Blackeyed Bulbuls beat the sparrows to the bird-table these days, but still retain a position in the wild where man does not assist. Insects, some snatched in flight, and wild fruits keep them fed.

These birds are conspicuous but their lightweight cup-nest high in a tree is not often found.

29 Cheerful Commoners in Residence

65 Kurrichane Thrush

Turdus libonyana
R576

Similar birds
Olive Thrush R577

A garden with big, well-foliaged trees and a little wildness left, is where you meet the Kurrichane Thrush. This bird, discreetly clad in sombre grey gently warmed with orange, takes its name from a place which is no more. Bold cheek-stripes like mascara which has run, flank a white throat and distinguish this thrush from 'look-alikes'. An orange beak is used to lay bare the creatures beneath fallen leaves.

Leaves warm from decay provide a niche for spiders, worms and snails. Here too the pupae for the new season's insects are stored until the weather warms. These things and more the thrush finds for food.

In a thick-branch fork, a bowl nest is moulded and remains unseen until gaping, orange mouths project in anticipation of food.

30 Modest Residents of Bush and Garden

66 Familiar Chat

Cercomela familiaris
R589

Similar birds
Mountain Chat
R586

The Familiar Chat with a door-to-door salesman's cheek is a farmyard acquaintance; this drab, little bird will become exceedingly familiar. Almost every movement, except flight, is punctuated by wing flicks. A T-patterned, orange tail hinged to an orange rump is lifted and lowered in a gesture reserved for a conductor's baton. The rostrum for all this activity is anything which is higher than everything else in the vicinity, be it a wall, a windmill or just a biggish stone where terrain is flat.

Insects are chats' food and are the draw card to farm buildings with animals around. Bird-table fare like suet and bone-meal would be a bonus.

A hole is for nest-building; where the hole is situated is not strictly specified. Bright eggs of blue, speckled with rust, are laid in a cup nest built on a small stone base from any cosy junk at hand.

30 Modest Residents of Bush and Garden

67 Cape Robin
Cossypha caffra
R601

Similar birds
Whitethroated
Robin R602

The Cape Robin is a bird of the undergrowth; whether it be yours or growing wild does not matter much to this bird, which is well adapted to gardens. The meeting will be in a shady place with a retreat near at hand. Bold hops on legs quite thin, a jerking orange tail and a striped head quizzically cocked are Cape Robin characteristics you can hardly miss. In keeping with robin tradition, it also wears an orange patch extending from throat to chest.

Of the myriad of tiny creatures that shelter in the shrubbery, this robin eats most of them, and berries beside.

One does not know the criteria for nest-site selection that instinct demands, but items of junk seem to meet them in the world of Cape Robins. Tin cans, flower pots and piles of brushwood have been used to conceal a cup nest lined with horsehair.

30 Modest Residents of Bush and Garden

68 Titbabbler

Parisoma subcaeruleum
R621

Similar birds
Spotted Flycatcher
R689

A churring call in a thicket, perhaps followed by more melodious singing, could be the prelude to an introduction to a Titbabbler. Peer into the fabric of densely woven branches and look for a small, dull-grey bird with a reddish patch beneath its tail. Confirm your acquaintance by the spotted chin and the white tip to a dark tail. You may even get a glimpse of pale titbabbler eyes. A mate similarly grey may be near at hand, but titbabblers are loners much of the time.

The Titbabbler creeps to feed deep in the denseness of shrubbery. Here insects and spiders are stripped from twigs with a small beak, and small fruits are eaten if found on the way.

A cup formed from fine grasses and tiny roots is bound with spider web to make it strong, and to secure it to twigs in a bush. Small white eggs lightly dabbed with brown and slate are laid.

31 Small Dwellers of Scrub and Woodland

69 Neddicky
Cisticola fulvicapilla
R681

Similar birds
Lazy Cisticola R679

The Neddicky has slipped into a narrow niche left by the birds of the trees and those of the ground, and this is where you can make contact. Muted shades of grey and brown drawn from the habitat are mingled to produce an austere image, relieved only by the warm brown on the head. Spindly pinkish legs thinner than matches are the most obvious feature of this humbly presented bird. The male takes a tree-top perch to sing in summer.

Neddicky food is small insects that live in the twilight zone of shrubbery for at least part of their lives.

Fine dry grasses, mingled with spider web and formed into a hollow ball, make the nest that is merged into the low-level habitat of this nondescript but welcome little bird, which sometimes comes to gardens.

31 Small Dwellers of Scrub and Woodland

70 Blackchested Prinia

Prinia flavicans
R685

Similar birds
Tawnyflanked
Prinia R683

The Blackchested Prinia and other prinias have eloquent tails which wag, flick and cock in various directions to distinguish them from a host of other little brown birds which also have shares in a low bush habitat. A bold black band worn about the chest in summer will tell you which prinia you have met, because most have lemon yellow on breast and belly, and plain browny shades above. Longish legs, pinkish and fragile-looking, are also standard accessories.

Look for the prinias just before the rose bushes are pruned and sterilised with spray; they could be there before you, delicately removing dormant insect pests.

In shrubbery quite near the house you may find the woven-pouch nest of a prinia, seeking the security offered by human presence.

31 Small Dwellers of Scrub and Woodland

71 Fiscal Flycatcher

Sigelus silens
R698

Similar birds
Fiscal Shrike R732

This is a friendly flycatcher which embodies a robin-like charm and cockiness as it takes over a section of your garden. The Fiscal Flycatcher is the sort of bird you could easily strike up an acquaintance with while drinking tea on the patio. The male is immaculate in black and white; his mate makes do with a toil-worn equivalent. Any similarity these birds share with the Fiscal Shrike is no more than skin-deep, and perhaps coincidental.

Actual flycatching is seldom done. Insects are usually picked up from the ground in sallies from a garden bench or other convenient perch. Berries, foreign and local, are additional fare, further sweetened with aloe nectar in winter.

The Fiscal Flycatcher nest is a bowl of twigs and grass trimmed with lichen and warmly lined with down, placed in a fork in a tree or palm.

32 Feathered Flycatching Friends of the Gardener

72 Paradise Flycatcher

Terpsiphone viridis
R710

Similar birds
Bluemantled
Flycatcher R708

The male Paradise Flycatcher is an orangy wisp of a bird which flits and flirts with feverish activity in a summertime venture to reproduce its kind. His mate is more modest and does not sport a tail; together they form an intimate partnership with a territory which may include the immediate environs of your house. A meeting is inevitable. The waxy blue eye-trim and a dark crest with a sheen are unique complements to the russet upper plumage and tail.

Insects are the staple fare for flycatchers, and these are whisked from the air in a quick swoop which starts and finishes on a perch without any apparent hesitation.

The woven cobweb and lichen nest-cup is merged with a twiggy fork at the end of a branch. Tiny eggs are laid with mutual ado and up to three baby flycatchers may crowd the tiny nest.

32 Feathered Flycatching Friends of the Gardener

73 Cape Wagtail

Motacilla capensis
R713

Similar birds
African Pied Wagtail R711

This matey little walking bird with a jaunty, wagging tail is making a comeback to gardens and parks after an apparent decline, perhaps caused by insecticides. The appeal of the Cape Wagtail lies in its mannerisms rather than in its plumage, which is a dull blend of greys; it almost invites your attention as it tamely walks in front of you, zigzagging to pick up an insect on the way.

Wagtails feed as they walk, but also take little forms of life from shallow water, while stone-hopping. Freshly mown grass offers easy pickings.

A weedy bundle with neatly finished cup is the Cape Wagtail's nest, which may be constructed anywhere – from in an old wheelbarrow to within the shelter of a dense creeper. Mottled yellowish eggs are brooded by both parents. This parental partnership continues with feeding of the young.

33 Garden Tail-waggers and Rural Kin

74 Richard's Pipit

Anthus novaeseelandiae
R716

Similar birds
Longbilled Pipit
R717

The meeting is a difficult one; pipit species are as indistinguishable as the dry, winter grasses that make up much of the habitat of these ground-loving birds.

Richard's Pipit is one you are most likely to encounter because it occurs throughout the country. Running, then pausing to look with a tail-dipping gesture, is the custom of this pipit; if alarmed it perches on post or bush; in display it flies high, calling in bursts of monotonous song.

Food of pipits is mainly insects taken from the ground. Fire-ravaged veld is an attraction as an easy source of food.

Tucked under a tussock of grass, well-hidden from view, you may find a Richard's Pipit nest. Three white eggs heavily speckled with shades of the veld make up a normal clutch.

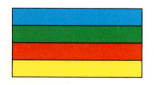

33 Garden Tail-waggers and Rural Kin

75 Orange-throated Longclaw

Macronyx capensis
R727

Similar birds
Yellowthroated Longclaw R728

The Orangethroated Longclaw is like a stocky, oversized pipit from the back; move round to the front and you will see your mistake. The bird you have just met has a bright orange throat, rimmed in black from chin to chest. The chest and belly are deep yellow. Strong legs are for running in treeless grassland or vlei, and the feet are oversized with long, sharp claws. In the fluttering flight of display the bird rises then drops again quickly to the ground, as though it had forgotten to do something before leaving.

Termites scratched from their nests are part of the longclaw's diet together with other insect denizens of the grassland.

The Orangethroated Longclaw's nest is a heavy cup formed from coarse grass, then tidily lined with fine material. The whole structure is blended into a tuft of grass and masterfully hidden.

33 Garden Tail-waggers and Rural Kin

76 Fiscal Shrike

Lanius collaris
R732

Similar birds
Southern Boubou
R736
Fiscal Flycatcher
R698

The Fiscal Shrike will often arrange the meeting with you to proclaim a territory. White front and black back with bold white V from shoulder to shoulder are characteristics not easily confused; the heavy head and hooked beak complete the picture. From a tall perch this aggressive shrike will swoop down to catch its prey on the ground or fly to a similar high spot, skimming the ground in between. At times it will sing its mixed-up, unmelodious song, with tail held askew.

Live prey is the Fiscal's diet. Birds, animals and insects are killed and sometimes impaled on wire or thorns for later eating. Hence the name Jackie Hangman.

Grass, roots, rags and rubbish are used to make a cup nest in a dense bush. Heavily marked, pale blue eggs are laid with little regard to season.

34 Urban Hangmen and Bush Relatives

77 Crimson-breasted Shrike

Laniarius atrococcineus
R739

Similar birds
Southern Boubou
R736

From a distance the Crimsonbreasted Shrike seems like a great drop of blood against the muted background of its bush habitat. Nearer, the intense black upper parts, relieved by white wing-stripes, set off the brilliant red of breast and throat. An unforgettable meeting ensues, for this shrike is one of our most beautiful birds, and one where beauty is not limited to one partner. This shrike has not adapted to man and is vulnerable to modification of its dry, thorn-bush habitat.

Crimsonbreasted Shrikes often run about at ground level to find their insect food, but are really birds of the trees.

Bark stripped from special trees makes the outer structure of an open nest, which is bound into place with spider web and then finally finished with a smooth, fibrous lining.

78 Bokmakierie
Telophorus zeylonus
R746

Similar birds
Greyheaded Bush Shrike R751

For those who have lived with Bokmakieries all their lives, the vibrant duet pouring from two olive-green birds is perhaps commonplace. For those who hear it for the first time, or again after some years, it is the sound of a special place. It is uttered with enthusiastic abandon from prominent perches some distance apart. Make the acquaintance of Bokmakieries in a garden using a bird-table with bone-meal or suet at hand. Note the bold black band starkly laid across the intense yellow of underparts and throat of this bird; the tail is black with feathers tipped in yellow and is easily recognisable in flight.

Insects and other small creatures, including birds, are part of a typical shrike menu.

A shrike-style nest is placed fairly low in a dense bush, and blue-green eggs with brown spots are usually laid in summer.

34 Urban Hangmen and Bush Relatives

79 European Starling

Sturnus vulgaris
R757

Similar birds
Indian Mynah R758

The European Starling is a last-century import which started out in Cape Town, toured the Garden Route and eventually reached Durban, with pioneering zeal. Those who must endure the messy invasion of city buildings and trees by a hoard of roosting starlings all calling at once, would surely opt for repatriation. The bird is plain by local glossy starling standards; at best its plumage is only a spotty sheen. You could meet this bird with a few of its mates while they are strutting about, or probing worms from the lawn.

Diet is based on an 'anything goes' principle with fruits, including grapes, quite high on the priority list. The questionable popularity of starlings wanes further in fruit-growing circles.

These starlings build a straggly bowl in a hole under eaves or elsewhere close to man, to raise their young.

35 City-dwelling Imports

80 Indian Mynah

Acridotheres tristis
R758

Similar birds
European Starling
R757

The Indian Mynah is an unwitting immigrant from the East, which seems to thrive where man has downgraded the natural habitats. If mynahs are around, you will be meeting them; of that you can be sure. A chocolate bird with a black head and breast and patches of white on its wings, will call with a mate and a proprietorial air. A yellow beak with matching eye-trim, and strong yellow legs for moving boldly, proclaim this to be a starling with a difference. The discordant muddle of sound that makes up the mynah's song may become a regular feature as urbanisation progresses.

Mynahs will eat almost anything and will dominate a bird-table where they can throw their weight around.

A heap of grass, twigs and a selection of local bits of rubbish, is hidden in a hole almost anywhere to serve as a nest for up to six mynah chicks.

35 City-dwelling Imports

81 Plumcoloured Starling

Cinnyricinclus leucogaster
R761

Similar birds
None

The male Plumcoloured Starling is richly clad in a mantle of shimmering bishop's-purple with a hood to match; pristine white underparts and a golden eye complete the dandy image. He will be the contact at the first meeting; his mate in spotty brown and white will be ignored, until she is introduced. At times there may be several male birds harmoniously exploring a rural garden, yet on another occasion they may be thrashing each other in the dirt, oblivious of damage to gorgeous finery.

Fruits plucked from the wild figs which grow in the bushveld habitat of this bird contribute to a summertime diet.

Wild trees with holes are the preferred nesting place for Plumcoloured Starlings, but a rusty fence post leaning from neglect will also do. Fresh foliage is regularly placed in the nest in a ritual we cannot explain.

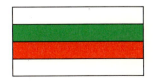

82 Glossy Starling

Lamprotornis nitens
R764

Similar birds
Redwinged Starling
R769

The Glossy Starling is totally enclosed in metallic blue-green. Bright orange eyes set like jewels contrast vividly with dark plumage to create a distinctive bird, easily recognised at that vital first meeting. You too could have a few of these shiny birds at home in your garden with a bird-table and bone-meal, in the winter months. Its gentle, rolling call-note is uttered as it flies off, as if in farewell.

Insects taken while striding on the ground, fruit both wild and otherwise, and aloe nectar make up a varied year-round diet.

Holes natural and man-made, in trees and almost anywhere else, are used by Glossy Starlings to make a nest. Padding is added, which may include cast-off snake skins for some strange reason, and then the eggs are laid. Brothers and sisters of earlier broods help with the feeding of the young.

36 Shiny Birds of Bush and Berg

83 Redwinged Starling

Onychognathus morio
R769

Similar birds
Pied Starling R759

A flock of glossy black birds cascading from cliffs with wings aflame is a nostalgic reflection on a meeting with Redwinged Starlings long ago. This is a bird of the mountains which has adapted to buildings and integrated with the ways of man without losing its dignity. Its mellow whistling call of communication transcends the oppressive noise of traffic. Close-up the plumage is seen to be very deep blue with a gloss; main wing feathers are red brown. It is the biggest of all our starlings.

Ripe fruit in the garden draws the Redwinged Starlings in flocks, but ticks taken from cattle are also acceptable.

The site is a ledge on a cliff or building sheltered from above; the nest is of mud formed into a bowl with grassy material and then lined. Three elongated blue-green eggs with freckles form the usual clutch.

36 Shiny Birds of Bush and Berg

84 Redbilled Oxpecker

Buphagus erythrorhynchus
R772

Similar birds
Yellowbilled Oxpecker R771

These strange birds of Africa are locked in partnership with big game animals in wild places, and easy-to-reach domestic stock, where habitat is shared with man. You could meet one or more Redbilled Oxpeckers on the long neck of a giraffe in a game reserve, and watch them cling and clamber with magnetic tenacity, propped on their tails which are suitably stiffened. Plumage is modest in shades of brown to buff; a red bill and a yellow-rimmed eye add colour to a drab oddity.

Ticks are for eating in the oxpecker's book, and these are what is looked for while creeping about using sharp claws to maintain a grip. Wounds may also be sampled as a variation to invertebrate protein.

A hole in a tree is needed by oxpeckers to nest upon a cup of hair from a convenient host. Nestlings are fed by the parents and volunteers.

37 Gamecreepers of the Wild

85 Cape Sugarbird

Promerops cafer
R773

Similar birds
Gurney's Sugarbird
R774

The sugarbirds seem to be big sunbirds fitted with long, soft tails, yet in fact they are an unusual family all on their own. A meeting in the fynbos of the Cape will be with the Cape Sugarbird perched upon a protea or bottle-brush in full flower. Whisking tails and flicking wings are part of a chasing routine to tell other sugarbirds where territories begin and end. Their streaked plumage is mainly brown and white with shades in between, except for a yellow patch beneath the tail.

Nectar is probed from flowers with a long beak. But tiny creatures encountered on the way are also eaten in a kind of sweet-and-sour diet.

A cup of a nest is messily formed from twigs, grass and other bits, in a protea tree. The shiny brown fluff of wind-borne protea seeds is lightly bound inside where the eggs will lie.

38 Nectar-loving Flower Birds

86 Whitebellied Sunbird

Nectarinia talatala
R787

Similar birds
Dusky Sunbird
R788

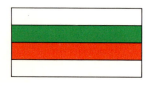

The Whitebellied Sunbird is a sipper of nectar from tubular flowers, and this is where you will meet. The male wears a hood and cloak made from feather platelets of shimmering metallic green, and a band of purple to separate the white of the belly. His mate is drab. Frenetic is the pace which this little creature sets as it feeds from the nectar of aloes, races after other sunbirds and sings constantly in sweet little notes.

The long, curved beak with a tongue to match draws the nectar from the flowers, and provides a sharp tool for short circuiting when the flowers are too deep. It is also used for providing vital protein-rich insects to feed the young.

A raggedy nest in the form of a purse opens on the side with fitted porch. In sunbird society the female must assemble the nest material and bind it with spider web to a branch.

38 Nectar-loving Flower Birds

87 Black Sunbird

Nectarinia amethystina
R792

Similar birds
Scarletchested Sunbird R791

The Black Sunbird is mostly black at the first meeting. A patch of shimmering green laid in tiny metallic platelets upon the head later catches your eye as this nectar-loving bird hovers, caught by the sun, at an aloe in your garden. When stretching to reach the most succulent flower, shiny scales of metallic purple glisten at the throat and rump. Purple epaulettes on the wings may be seen sometimes. True to sunbird custom the female plays the poor relation in humble plumage.

Sunbirds are birds of the flowers and the presence of the Black Sunbird depends on what is on offer at the time. Honeysuckle, red-hot poker or poinsettia, it does not matter; indigenous or exotic nectar seems to taste the same.

An oval nest of grass, leaves and bark with lichen trim is bound with the web of spiders to hang from a branch in a tree or creeper.

88 Cape White-eye

Zosterops pallidus
R796

Similar birds
Yelloweyed Canary
R869

The meeting with Cape White-eyes will be a group affair at your place. The venue could be a full-flowering aloe, a feeder filled with bone-meal, or no more than a leaking tap on a hot summer's day. Friendly little birds, with a fitting sweet trilling call, twist and twirl and eat at an angle, while you watch and wonder at such tireless energy. These little, greenish yellow creatures with eyes ringed in white, bathe in the belly of an aloe leaf after rain and sup the nectar from flowers by puncturing the base.

Food is anything sweet, and insects and spiders besides. Juicy fruits and succulent flowers, honeydew from the aphids on your roses, and probably the insects themselves go together in a fun diet for white-eyes.

Gently cradled in a horizontal fork a tiny cup nest, impeccably finished, holds two or three pale shaded eggs from early spring onwards.

38 Nectar-loving Flower Birds

89 Cape Sparrow

Passer melanurus
R803

Similar birds
House Sparrow R801
Greyheaded Sparrow R804

You don't meet Cape Sparrows, you unwittingly and sometimes unwillingly, mingle with them almost every day. They are liberally sprinkled on lawns in parks, at home and among factories. There are even sparrows that wander the stark streets, urchin-like, smog-stained and dull, living off the rubbish people drop. The male sparrow, wearing black on head and breast with white C's hooked behind the eyes, is a familiar bird. His russet and white trim is muted in his mate, who looks like a foreign relative.

Food is seeds if seeds are there, but almost anything else is will do. Fresh young shoots are delicacies when the going is tough.

The sparrow nest is a mess, hollow and cosy. Often these heaps of grass and rubbish encroach under eaves or tangle with telephone wires.

39 Seed-eaters in the Garden

90 Cape Weaver

Ploceus capensis
R813

Similar birds
Spectacled Weaver
R810

Male Cape Weavers emerge to greet the spring in special courting attire. You will recognise this weaver when you meet, by the male's head of orangy brown, merging with bright yellow on chest and belly. Lightly marked yellow-green colours back and tail. Pale yellow eyes complete the theme. His mate remains in modest winter shades of olive, grey and white. The harsh, penetrating call of the male vocalising his ardour matches the heat of a summer day.

In winter time when plumage is drab the Cape Weaver supplements a seedy diet with the nectar from aloes and erythrinas, often eating the flowers as well.

Males take many mates and weave kidney-shaped nests in reeds and trees, with water nearby. A fickle female must approve both nest and site before lining and laying can start.

39 Seed-eaters in the Garden

91 Masked Weaver

Ploceus velatus
R814

Similar birds
Spottedbacked Weaver R811

Masked Weavers hang their round-bellied, woven nests from branches of trees in urban gardens, as frequently as they hang them in the veld these days. Stripping leaves from the tree around the nest site, practised by these birds spoils the tree and the meeting at times. Would this custom discourage snakes? The male weaver wears a distinctive black mask in sharp contrast to the rich shades of yellow which dominate the rest of its summer plumage. Eyes are red jewels set in black. Mates are wooed with nest-hanging displays and song described as swizzling.

Weavers are seed-eaters and so is this one, with an added taste for insects, nectar and flowers.

Nesting is a speculative exercise conducted by the male with feverish zest. Each effort is inspected by a nondescript mate, and those not accepted are destroyed by the creator in a frenzy.

39 Seed-eaters in the Garden

92 Red Bishop

Euplectes orix
R824

Similar birds
Redshouldered
Widow R828

You should meet the Red Bishop on his territory down in the reeds, where sectional title and polygamy combine. Watch the stick-puppet display on the end of a reed where out-thrust chest, splendid in deep-pile black, counters the fluffed, vivid scarlet of rump and belly in a bobbing dance. See the fiery puff-ball mark out what is his in slow-motion flight with wings buzzing. The streaky brown females potter unresponsive in the reeds below. It is a summertime affair and the reed-bed will close down like a theatre, when the players don winter browns.

Bishops are designed as seed-eaters, but feed young on insects to supply protein. Wintertime flocks of hundreds of birds ravage wheat and other grain. Nests are woven from strips of leaf cut from the reeds by the male. The interior decorating is females' work as are incubation and feeding of the young.

40 Summertime Bishops and Widows of the Vlei

93 Golden Bishop
Euplectes afer
R826

Similar birds
Yellowrumped Widow R827

Golden Bishops are birds of the grasses and weeds that grow thick and rank in places that are wet. There the males gather and subdivide habitat into territorial compartments. Like feathered facsimiles of giant bumble-bees, they float with beating wings, singing a clockwork song. The male Golden Bishop is mainly yellow above and mostly black below. Females are brown and streaked to confuse those who would distinguish them from brown counterparts of other species.

These bishops feed upon the seeds of grasses as the heads form in the fabric of their chosen habitat. Yet they prescribe an insect diet for their nestlings.

Nests are woven deep in the grass close to the ground so that they mingle with the vegetation and are not easy to find. Eggs are a spotted design exclusive to the species.

40 Summertime Bishops and Widows of the Vlei

94 Redcollared Widow

Euplectes ardens
R831

Similar birds
Longtailed Widow
R832

This is another widow in black you can meet in the vlei when summer is full. The long, black tail feathers which seem to have been gathered in a bunch, are hung out to flutter from a perch as the black male bird surveys his domain. Deep in the grass brown females hatch their eggs and feed their young content in sharing a gorgeous mate, whose only concession to colour is a low-slung slash of scarlet on his throat. As his ardour wells the male widow crooks his tail and floats over the grass with wings beating fast. The in-flight song is one some insects might sing.

Seeds and insects are the food of this bird and it too will swell the flocks of grain-seeking birds when the vleis turn yellow.

The woven grass nest follows widow tradition, and is lined with the heads of fine grasses. Pale eggs, heavily marked, are laid in threes.

40 Summertime Bishops and Widows of the Vlei

95 Longtailed Widow

Euplectes progne
R832

Similar birds
Redcollared Widow R831

The Longtailed Widow is the biggest of the widows you will meet. It is a bird of wide-open grasslands. Plumage is heavy black except for the bold red wing-patches underlined with white. A long, loosely gathered tail cascades down with the bird at rest. In the inverted-question-mark courtship display, tail feathers flare and bow, and floppy wings respond to an irregular rhythm while the bird moves slowly across its territory. Summer black is shed for winter, together with the long tail.

These birds of the grass eat seeds, and their roadside foraging in groups with long tails dragging cannot fail to draw attention.

A bundle of fine grass-heads drawn together to form a ball, is deeply concealed in a clump of living grass to serve as a nest in the polygamous community where females dominate the domestic scene.

40 Summertime Bishops and Widows of the Vlei

96 Blue Waxbill

Uraeginthus angolensis
R844

Similar birds
None

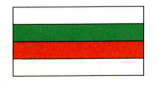

These pastel-shaded, little seed-eating birds are part of the garden scene in the north and east of the country, and there is little difficulty in striking up a relationship with a local group. Sky blue plumage is water-coloured on rump and tail, face and breast. Warm brown on the back completes the muted finery of this friendly little bird.

In the dryness of winter they gather in flocks to clear up the seeds the grass has let fall, and then at appointed times gather to drink at quiet, shallow places by a dam or stream.

Blue Waxbill nests are conspicuous, untidy balls of grass suitably lined to hold tiny white eggs. Beware intruders, because there is often a wasp nest in the immediate vicinity, as if a security arrangement had been negotiated by the birds prior to building their nest. One wonders if the wasps get anything from the deal?

41 Little Birds of the Grass

97 Common Waxbill

Estrilda astrild
R846

Similar birds
Jameson's
Firefinch R841

These are tiny birds of tall grass and rushes which stray to gardens that are suitably wild. You could get acquainted over a feeding device laced with small seed, but are more likely to meet where grass is long. A closer look transforms a little brown bird into a finely finished work of art. A warm wash of red glows on the belly, and modest plumage above and below has been barred as though with the finest sable brush. The small beak is tinted bright red and the same colour has been neatly applied to the feathers round the tiny eye. A jet-black patch under the longish tail finishes a beautiful little creature.

Fine seeds from the grassy heads or picked from the ground are waxbill food, but insects are added.

A double-storey nest made from fine grasses with a short tunnel entrance is merged with a tussock at ground level.

41 Little Birds of the Grass

98 Pintailed Whydah

Vidua macroura
R860

Similar birds
Shafttailed Whydah R861

The male Pintailed Whydah is a summertime character that appears on the stage strikingly costumed in black and white, with a long, black tail extension neatly formed from four slender feathers. A red beak completes the picture of a lively and aggressive small bird. Up to half a dozen heavily striped females in shades of brown are usually in attendance. The courtship display embodies an action where the male moves up and down in the air and circles as though tugging at a spring-loaded line, while long tail feathers rise and fall rhythmically.

Seed is what draws this whydah to your bird-table, but insects also feature on the menu.

The Pintailed Whydah is an arch-parasite to similar-sized birds. Members of his harem cunningly substitute their own eggs one at a time for those of their chosen host. The young whydah grows with its nestfellows without aggression.

42 Polygamous Parasites at your Feeding Tray

99 Yelloweyed Canary

Serinus mozambicus
R869

Similar birds
Yellow Canary
R878

Sweet, intermittent notes trickling from big trees after a thunderstorm has left everything wet, seem as crystal clear as the raindrops themselves. This could be your introduction to the Yelloweyed Canary, a local relative of the domestic songster. It is a small bird generally yellow on face, breast and belly, and streaky patterned green on the back. When you get closer look for the black lines from the chin, which look like the hanging ends of a long moustache. These canaries travel in groups, unobtrusive yet making an attractive contribution to a garden.

Food is mainly seed, but sweet flowers and insects are also included.

A small cup of grass and other plants, neatly bound with spider web and then carefully lined, is the kind of nest you would expect this sweet songster to have.

43 *Mellow Songsters of Garden and the Wild*

100 Rock Bunting

Emberiza tahapisi
R886

Similar birds
Cape Bunting R885

The Rock Bunting shares the country with the Cape Bunting with an overlap in the eastern parts. Your meeting with a Rock Bunting may be purely coincidental, because this small bird does not make its presence felt. A brownish bird retreating with undulating flight from a bare patch on an old, cultivated land and settling off the ground some distance away, is all you may see at first. Get a little closer to see a bird beautifully marked in shades of the veld. Warm cinnamon tones of breast and belly are offset by the heavily patterned brown of the back, but it is the white striped black of head and throat that is the bunting trade mark.

Seeds and insects from a dry habitat are bunting food.

A bunting nest is a cup of grass in a bed of sticks, upon the ground, half-hidden by a stone or a dry clump of vegetation.

43 Mellow Songsters of Garden and the Wild

Index

Babbler, Arrowmarked 63 *(Norman Elwell)*
Barbet, Blackcollared 55 *(Geoff McIlleron)*
  Crested 56 *(Norman Elwell)*
Bee-eater, Little 49 *(Norman Ellwell)*
Bishop, Golden 93 *(Geoff McIlleron)*
  Red 92 *(Geoff McIlleron)*
Bokmakierie 78 *(Norman Elwell)*
Bulbul, Blackeyed 64 *(Geoff McIlleron)*
Bunting, Rock 100 *(Geoff McIlleron)*

Canary, Yelloweyed 99 *(Geoff McIlleron)*
Chat, Familiar 66 *(Norman Elwell)*
Coot, Redknobbed 6 *(Norman Elwell)*
Cormorant, Reed 5 *(Norman Elwell)*
Coucal, Burchell's 37 *(Geoff McIlleron)*
Crane, Blue 13 *(Norman Elwell)*
Crow, Pied 62 *(Vic Hards)*
Cuckoo, Diederik 36 *(Geoff McIlleron)*
  Redchested 35 *(Norman Elwell)*

Dabchick 4 *(Norman Elwell)*
Dikkop, Spotted 30 *(Geoff McIlleron)*
Dove, Cape Turtle 32 *(Norman Elwell)*
  Laughing 33 *(Norman Elwell)*
Drongo, Forktailed 60 *(Geoff McIlleron)*
Duck, Yellowbilled 18 *(Tom Spence)*

Eagle, African Fish 23 *(Geoff McIlleron)*
  Black 22 *(Norman Elwell)*
Egret, Cattle 9 *(Norman Elwell)*

Flamingo, Greater 16 *(Norman Elwell)*
Flycatcher, Fiscal 71 *(Will Nichol)*
Flycatcher, Paradise 72 *(Geoff McIlleron)*
Francolin, Coqui 24 *(Norman Elwell)*
  Swainson's 25 *(Tom Spence)*

Gannet, Cape 3 *(Norman Elwell)*
Goose, Egyptian 17 *(Norman Elwell)*
Guineafowl, Helmeted 26 *(Geoff McIlleron)*
Gull, Greyheaded 2 *(Norman Elwell)*
  Kelp 1 *(Norman Elwell)*

Hamerkop 10 *(Norman Elwell)*
Heron, Blackheaded 8 *(Norman Elwell)*
  Grey 7 *(Norman Elwell)*
Hoopoe 51 *(Geoff McIlleron)*
Hornbill, Ground 54 *(Norman Elwell)*
  Yellowbilled 53 *(Geoff McIlleron)*

Ibis, Hadeda 15 *(Norman Elwell)*
  Sacred 14 *(Norman Elwell)*

Kingfisher, Brownhooded 48 *(Geoff McIlleron)*
  Malachite 47 *(Geoff Lockwood)*
  Pied 46 *(Geoff Lockwood)*
Kite, Blackshouldered 21 *(Tom Spence)*
Korhaan, Black 27 *(Norman Elwell)*

Lark, Rufousnaped 59 *(Geoff McIlleron)*
Longclaw, Orangethroated 75 *(Geoff McIlleron)*
Lourie, Grey 34 *(Norman Elwell)*

Mousebird, Speckled 45 *(Norman Elwell)*
Mynah, Indian 80 *(Geoff McIlleron)*

Neddicky 69 *(Geoff McIlleron)*
Nightjar, Fierynecked 41 *(Geoff Lockwood)*

Oriole, Blackheaded 61 *(Geoff McIlleron)*
Owl, Barn 38 *(Norman Elwell)*
  Pearlspotted 39 *(Geoff McIlleron)*
  Spotted Eagle 40 *(Tom Spence)*
Oxpecker, Redbilled 84 *(Geoff McIlleron)*

Pigeon, Rock 31 *(Peter Ginn)*
Pipit, Richard's 74 *(Geoff Lockwood)*
Plover, Crowned 29 *(Norman Elwell)*
  Threebanded 28 *(Norman Elwell)*

Prinia, Blackchested 70 *(Geoff McIlleron)*

Robin, Cape 67 *(Norman Elwell)*
Roller, Lilacbreasted 50 *(Norman Elwell)*

Secretarybird 19 *(Norman Elwell)*
Shrike, Crimsonbreasted 77 *(Geoff McIlleron)*
   Fiscal 76 *(Geoff McIlleron)*
Sparrow, Cape 89 *(Geoff McIlleron)*
Starling, European 79 *(Nico Myburgh)*
   Glossy 82 *(Norman Elwell)*
   Plumcoloured 81 *(Geoff McIlleron)*
   Redwinged 83 *(Peter Barachievy)*
Stork, Abdim's 12 *(Peter Ginn)*
   White 11 *(Norman Elwell)*
Sugarbird, Cape 85 *(Norman Elwell)*
Sunbird, Black 87 *(Geoff McIlleron)*
   Whitebellied 86 *(Geoff McIlleron)*
Swallow, European 43 *(Geoff McIlleron)*
   Lesser Striped 44 *(Norman Elwell)*

Swift, Whiterumped 42 *(John Bunning)*

Thrush, Kurrichane 65 *(Norman Elwell)*
Titbabbler 68 *(Norman Elwell)*

Vulture, Cape 20 *(Norman Elwell)*

Wagtail, Cape 73 *(Norman Elwell)*
Waxbill, Blue 96 *(Norman Elwell)*
   Common 97 *(Norman Elwell)*
Weaver, Cape 90 *(Nico Myburgh)*
   Masked 91 *(Norman Elwell)*
White-eye, Cape 88 *(Geoff McIlleron)*
Whydah, Pintailed 98 *(Peter Ginn)*
Widow, Longtailed 95 *(Clive Hopcroft)*
   Redcollared 94 *(Geoff McIlleron)*
Woodhoopoe, Redbilled 52 *(Geoff McIlleron)*
Woodpecker, Cardinal 57 *(Geoff Lockwood)*
Wryneck, Redthroated 58 *(Geoff McIlleron)*

NOTE: The number shown against each bird name in the index corresponds with the number given to the bird in the individual descriptions. The name of the photographer who contributed the colour photograph of the particular bird follows the number.